7 Steps to Becoming FINANCIALLY Free WORKBOOK

CHRIST THE KING CHURCH
830 Elm Street
Denver, CO 80220

The information provided in these materials is not to be construed as investment advice. Under no circumstances does the information in this content represent a recommendation to buy, sell, or hold any security.

PHIL LENAHAN

7 Steps to Becoming FINANCIALLY Free

WORKBOOK

OUR SUNDAY VISITOR PUBLISHING DIVISION
OUR SUNDAY VISITOR, INC.
HUNTINGTON, IN 46750

Copyright © 2006 by Phil Lenahan
www.VeritasFinancialMinistries.com
Published 2006

11 10 09 08 07 06   2 3 4 5 6 7 8 9

Our Sunday Visitor Publishing Division
Our Sunday Visitor, Inc.
200 Noll Plaza
Huntington, IN 46750

ISBN-13: 978-1-59276-253-8
ISBN-10: 1-59276-253-0 (Inventory No. X304)

Cover design by Troy Lefevra
Interior design by Sherri L. Hoffman

PRINTED IN THE UNITED STATES OF AMERICA

TABLE OF CONTENTS

INTRODUCTION

The purpose of this workbook is to help you practically apply the material contained in the book *7 Steps to Becoming Financially Free*. While you can go through this workbook on your own, or with your spouse, I highly recommend going through it in a small-group study format. The small-group study is an ideal setting for learning these materials because of the mutual support that is given and received by you and the other participants. The group setting also helps you realize that you aren't the only one out there who has a bit to learn about managing your money, especially in light of your faith. Finally, it provides a great way to bring some needed accountability. As the saying goes, "you'll get out of it what you put into it." The small-group study provides that little bit of extra encouragement that many folks need to get all they can out of the materials. There is no need to worry that your personal financial situation will be open for others to see. There is no sharing of personal financial information during the small-group study.

The discussion topics in each of the sessions refer you to both the Bible and the *Catechism of the Catholic Church*. It is highly recommended that you own a copy of both. The Bible translation used is the *Catholic Edition of the Revised Standard Version of the Bible* (RSV). Many Bible quotations referred to in the sessions are included in the back of this book, along with answers to discussion topics.

You can find out more about the small group study and where the closest one is to you by logging on to www.VeritasFinancialMinistries.com.

BECOMING A STEWARD OF PROVIDENCE

PRE-SESSION ONE REQUIREMENTS

➤ Read the following from *7 Steps to Becoming Financially Free*: Introduction; Chapters 1 and 2.

➤ Complete the following session-one material in the workbook:
- ❑ Review goals for session.
- ❑ Answer discussion topics.
- ❑ Complete reading in practical-exercise section.
- ❑ Record daily spending for two weeks before starting session one using the Spending Diary (Form A in Appendix D). Instructions are at the end of session one.

GOALS — SESSION ONE

➤ Recognize how our faith intersects with our finances.

➤ Understand God's role and our role when it comes to money matters.

➤ Implementing a daily spiritual plan — time for exercise!

➤ Develop an understanding of where your money is going by beginning to record your spending using the Spending Diary.

OPENING PRAYER AND INTRODUCTORY VIDEO

Led by group leader.

1. **Read Isaiah 55:8-9.**

   Drawing on this verse and the readings from *7 Steps to Becoming Financially Free,* how does God's plan for our finances differ from the world's plan?

   _____

   _____

   _____

   _____

   _____

2. **Read the following references: Deuteronomy 10:14; 1 Chronicles 29:11-12; Psalm 24:1; 1 Corinthians 4:1-2; *Catechism* 2404; Luke 14:33.**

   How do the Scriptures and *Catechism* describe God's role when it comes to money? How is your role described? Consider the differences between being an owner and a steward. How should being a "Steward of Providence" impact how you prioritize the use of your resources?

   _____

   _____

   _____

   _____

   _____

3. Read the following references: John 3:16; Mark 8:36; Matthew 6:24; Job 1:21.

We know we can't take our material things with us when we die, yet we sometimes act as though we can. What did the Lord have to say about money and eternal life?

_____

_____

_____

_____

_____

4. Read the following references: Matthew 5:1-12; 5:48; _Catechism_ 2015 and 459; Matthew 7:24-27; John 2:5; 8:12; 12:26.

Jesus makes it clear that the way we can grow in our love of Him is to follow His teaching and His example. So often we think of freedom as the right to do what we want. True freedom is the call to do what we should. How can you know what you should do to become holy? How can applying Catholic principles to your finances lead you to a closer relationship with the Lord and help you reach your important goals in life?

_____

_____

_____

_____

_____

5. Can you relate to any of the money personality types in the book? What particular strengths and weaknesses do you see in yourself when it comes to handling money? (Group leaders will initiate this discussion.)

_____

_____

_____

_____

_____

6. **Read Ephesians 6:10-18; 1 Timothy 4:7-8; *Catechism* 1866.**
The *Catechism* lists the capital sins as pride, avarice, envy, wrath, lust, gluttony, and sloth or acedia. For most of us, one of these will be dominant. Can you relate to one in particular as your predominant fault? Describe how a daily spiritual plan will help you stay close to the Lord and overcome your predominant fault.

_____

_____

_____

_____

*T*he purpose of the 30-day spending diary is to help you understand where your money is going. If you faithfully do your homework, by the time you get to session three, you'll have a wealth of information about your spending patterns that will help you create an initial budget. For those of you participating in a small group, you'll want to start your Spending Diary (Form A in AppendixD) immediately after your orientation meeting. For those of you going through the workbook on your own, make sure you use the Spending Diary for four weeks before you complete session three. You'll start recording *every* purchase you make on a daily basis. Here are the steps you need to take.

- The first (and most important) step is to make sure you have a record of everything you spend money on. When you write a check to pay a regular bill, for example, your mortgage or utilities, save your copy of the bill as the receipt. For cash, debit card, or credit card purchases, you'll need to save the receipt from the store. That means getting a receipt for every purchase, even for a pack of gum. This may be a new behavior for you, but it will become a valuable habit very quickly. If you are unable to get a receipt for a purchase, you'll need to make one yourself. Write down the amount and what it was for on a small scrap of paper or back of a business card if you have to.

- You'll place the receipts for each week in a separate envelope. So get four envelopes and mark them week one through week four. You'll want to keep them all in one place (a drawer or small box works well).

- At the end of each week, grab a cup of coffee, tea, or lemonade and sit down to record your receipts on the Spending Diary. It's really very simple. Take out the appropriate week's envelope of receipts and fill out the date of the purchase, how you paid for it (cash, check, debit or credit card, bill pay), and note a brief description of "what" you purchased. Examples would be a cup of coffee, lunch, groceries etc. Then place the amount of the purchase under the most applicable spending category. Most category choices will be obvious, but here are a few suggestions for those that may not be quite so clear. You'll learn more about assigning to categories in session three.

  - Lattes, Meals Out, Cable TV – all go to Entertainment and Recreation
  - Haircuts, Cosmetics, Dry Cleaning, Pet Expenses – all to Miscellaneous

- Repeat this same process for weeks two through four until you have 30 days of spending history. This important information will be used when you create your first budget in a few sessions. Don't wait more than a week to record your expenses, otherwise the receipts will stack up and you'll feel overwhelmed. Some of you may even want to record them daily.

  If you are married, the spouse who has the greater eye for detail should be the one who handles the actual recording of the receipts in the Spending Diary. Just because one spouse handles the financial details doesn't let the other spouse off the hook! Both of you have to diligently save all of your receipts and plan on getting together each week to review your updated Spending Diary.

By completing your Spending Diary, you'll accomplish two things. First, you'll be getting practice at tracking your spending. Second, you'll probably find yourself surprised at where your money is going. Both of these are key building blocks as you begin the process of developing a financial plan. Review the sample spending diary below. It includes one week's worth of spending for three categories.

SAMPLE SPENDING DIARY					
Date	Pmt Type	Description	Groceries	Clothing	Entertainment and Recreation
1-Jun	Check	Cox Cable			67
2-Jun	Check	Food Giant—groceries	264		
3-Jun	Credit	Dillards—shoes and socks for kids		62	
3-Jun	Credit	Domino's Pizza—dinner			31
5-Jun	Credit	Dan's Drive Up Dairy—Milk	4		
6-Jun	Credit	Walgreens—soda	10		

HOMEWORK

➤ Create and start implementing your daily spiritual plan.

➤ Record daily spending on the Spending Diary.

"Keeping a home and a family is just as much a business as running a store; so why should it not be kept on a business basis? Many couples have had their eyes opened by keeping an itemized account of disbursements. They found that they had been extravagant without realizing it. But if keeping tab on one's expenses teaches economy, it should be done in every Christian home; for economy, supernaturalized, is nothing but the Christian virtue of moderation."

– THE CHRISTIAN HOME BY REV. CELESTINE STRUB, O.F.M.

7 STEPS TO BECOMING FINANCIALLY FREE

STEP ONE   Be a "Steward of Providence"

STEP TWO   Assess Where You Are – Develop a Plan

STEP THREE $2,000 Emergency Savings

STEP FOUR   Eliminate Debt – Accelerate It!

STEP FIVE   Rainy Day Fund – Six Months' Expenses

STEP SIX   Review Insurance and Estate Planning Needs

STEP SEVEN   Save and Invest with a Purpose

MARRIAGE AND MONEY
WORK: A PATH TO HOLINESS

PRE-SESSION TWO REQUIREMENTS

➤ Read the following from *7 Steps to Becoming Financially Free*: Chapters 3 and 5.

➤ Complete the following session-two material in the workbook:
  - ❏ Review goals for session.
  - ❏ Answer discussion topics.
  - ❏ Complete reading in practical exercise section.

GOALS — SESSION TWO

➤ Better recognize what it means to be faithful in your work and how to maintain proper balance between your faith, work, and family life.

➤ Recognize how different attitudes toward money between husband and wife impact the marriage relationship; understand how to develop unity in the marriage relationship with Christ at the center.

➤ Recognize the talents each spouse brings to the marriage. Determine which spouse is more suited to handling the day-to-day money issues.

➤ Understand how to develop a balance sheet and summary of debts.

➤ Set a regular schedule for your "Family Budget Meetings."

OPENING PRAYER AND INTRODUCTORY VIDEO

Led by group leader.

1. **Read the following references:** *Catechism* **1601, 1641, 1666.**

The *Catechism* describes marriage in beautiful terms. With the weakening of the family in our society over the last few decades, many people haven't had a good parental example to follow when it comes to family life, including how money was managed. Consider how money was viewed in your household when you were growing up. How has that impacted your attitude toward money today? Have your spouse do the same and share your thoughts.

_____

_____

_____

_____

_____

_____

2. **Read the following references: 1 Corinthians 13:1-13; Ephesians 5:21-33; Genesis 2:24; Mark 10:9.**

Given the fact that most spouses will have different perspectives on managing money, how can a Christian sense of unity be developed?

_____

_____

_____

_____

_____

_____

3. **Read 1 Corinthians 12:4-7.**

Take a moment to consider the gifts the Lord has given to you and describe at least two of them. If married, also describe two gifts your spouse has and share them with each other. Which of you is more suited to managing the day-to-day money issues?

_____

_____

_____

_____

_____

_____

4. **Read Psalm 32:8; 119:105; Proverbs 12:15; 13:10; 15:22.**

Good counsel is obviously very important, including God's counsel to us, and counsel between spouses. Even though one person will take primary responsibility for the day-to-day financial duties, why is it important that there be open communication between spouses? Describe how holding "Family Budget Meetings" and praying together beforehand can help foster good counsel.

_____

_____

_____

_____

_____

_____

5. Read the following references: *Christifideles Laici* 59 (in Appendix A); *Catechism* 2427; Psalm 127:1-2; Philippians 2:3-8.

Work is so much of who we are, yet we often fail to recognize the role that faith should have on our work. How should your faith influence your work? How can you become a more effective employee or employer by applying Catholic teaching in your work life?

_____

_____

_____

_____

_____

_____

6. Read the following references: Exodus 18:13-27; 20:9-11; *Catechism* 2184-2187.

Balancing our faith, family and work is an ongoing effort. Why is achieving this balance important? How well are you doing in maintaining such a balance?

_____

_____

_____

_____

_____

_____

Balance Sheet
Summary of Debts

The purpose of this exercise is to help you understand your current financial status. The tools you'll learn about and use for your homework assignment include a balance sheet and summary of debts.

Balance Sheet

A balance sheet is like a snapshot of your financial position at one point in time. It is simply a listing of your assets (what you own) and your liabilities (what you owe). Assets minus liabilities equals your net worth.

For most people, their balance sheet changes pretty dramatically during their lifetime. College students typically have almost no assets and often have student loans, so it's not unusual for them to have a negative net worth. A young married couple starting a family begins to add assets such as automobiles and their first home, but these normally come with a lot of debt attached. So the young couple's net worth doesn't change all that much in the early years.

As people get into their forties and fifties, it's important that their net worth grows sufficiently to meet upcoming needs, such as paying for college and retirement. While circumstances vary, it's not unusual for people in their retirement years to tap into their assets to meet day-to-day needs. This results in a declining net worth. Their goal would be to certainly have adequate resources to meet their retirement needs and to pass on a reasonable inheritance for their children.

So you can see, there really isn't one balance sheet that is standard for everyone. It depends on your stage in life and the responsibilities the Lord has entrusted to you. Let's make sure we understand the parts that make up the balance sheet:

Assets

Once again, an asset is simply something that you own. Assets are listed on the balance sheet at their fair market value, in other words, what they could be sold for today. We categorize assets on the balance sheet as follows:

- Cash and Cash Equivalents – these are assets that are readily converted into cash and include such things as checking accounts, savings accounts, and money-market funds. Money-market funds would normally be owned within the account you have with a stock-brokerage account. You can access it easily and without incurring a penalty for making an early withdrawal. These historically offer a higher rate than a money-market account with a traditional bank. However, times are changing, and some banks are offering competitive rates. Make sure you compare rates before deciding where to hold your cash equivalents. A good part of your rainy-day fund should be placed in your money market fund.

- The cash surrender value of permanent life insurance policies is a bit of an oddity. While in most circumstances, I recommend term insurance, some people already have policies with a cash value. You may decide to switch to term (make sure to have a new term policy in place before canceling your permanent policy), in which case the cash value can be used for other purposes, including paying down debt. If you plan on keeping your existing cash value policies, I would include the cash value under Invested Assets.

- Invested Assets – this category includes such things as certificates of deposit, stock, mutual funds, retirement plans, precious metals, investment real estate, vested pension benefits, ownership interest in closely held businesses, and other similar assets. The hallmark of these assets is that you are putting them to work so that they grow in value over time to help you meet your life's goals. They are not as easily converted to cash in the short term.

- Use Assets – this category includes your personal residence, automobiles, boats, and personal effects such as home furnishings and jewelry. Again, you should value them at the net price you could obtain for them today.

Liabilities

As noted above, when you have a liability, it means you owe a debt to someone. Sometimes the debt is secured by one of your assets (for example, your home or automobile). At other times, the debt is unsecured, meaning it is not tied to any of your assets (for example, credit-card debt and personal debt to friends and family). Debts are listed on the balance sheet at the amount you owe today. Here are some common types of liabilities:

- Mortgage and Home Equity Loans
- Automobile Loans
- Credit Cards and Installment Loans
- Student Loans
- Business Loans
- Other (Loans from Family and Friends; Retirement Plans; Life Insurance)

Net Worth

Net worth is the difference between assets and liabilities. It is an important measure that can reveal how well you are doing toward meeting your future financial needs.

Summary of Debts

The summary of debts is a supporting schedule for the balance sheet. This form provides all of the critical information relating to your debts — whom you owe money to, the current balance, number of payments remaining, interest rate, the minimum payment required, and a description of what it was that you purchased. This worksheet becomes very useful to help you start rapidly paying off your debts by creating your personal accelerator repayment plan (session four). You'll see how important it is for you to understand what the interest rate is that you are being charged on your debts. While you'll save more money paying down your highest interest-rate debts first, some people prefer the emotional boost they get from paying down smaller debts more quickly. You'll want to choose the method that works for you.

Let's Visit the Stewart Family

During the course of these sessions, we'll be visiting with the fictitious Stewart Family to see how they applied these tools in their circumstances. Let's take a look at their balance sheet and summary of debts (see "Sample Balance Sheet" on page 24 and "Sample Summary of Debts" on page 25). Tom and Patty did a good job of completing their forms. In reviewing the balance sheet below, you can see that their most significant asset is their house. With the exception of Tom's retirement plan from work, they have very little in the way of cash or investments. Their other assets consist of two cars and their home furnishings.

Tom's and Patty's liabilities consist of their mortgage, one auto loan, and credit-card debts. You can see that they owe $10,000 on credit cards, which are documented in greater detail on the summary of debts. The balance sheet shows the Stewarts have a net worth of $68,200. The Stewart's summary of debts shows a $200,000 mortgage, an auto loan of $10,000, and three credit cards with balances outstanding of $10,000, which matches the balance sheet total.

Now It's Your Turn

As part of your homework this next week, you'll complete your own personal balance sheet and summary of debts (using the blank forms in Appendix D or creating your balance sheet online at www.VeritasFinancialMinistries.com). On the balance sheet, list amounts for all assets and liabilities as of the most recent date. For example, use the current balance in your check register and balances from the most recent bank statements for savings accounts and investments. List the current value of your home, car, and home furnishings, and then enter the sum of all assets on the line titled "Total Assets."

For liabilities, begin with the summary of debts by listing all of the requested information related to each loan. This information should be available on the monthly statements from your lenders. If not, contact your lender to determine the necessary information. Once you have completed the summary of debts, transfer the amounts to the balance sheet by category of debt (for example mortgage, home-equity loan, auto loan, credit-card debt, etc.). The sum of these should be entered on the line "Total Liabilities." Total assets minus total liabilities equals net worth and should be entered on that line.

Once you have your information summarized, review your balance sheet in light of the 7 Steps to Becoming Financially Free. Do you have $2,000 set aside for an emergency fund? Do you have any consumer debt, such as credit cards or auto loans? Do you have rainy-day savings set aside above and beyond your $2,000 emergency fund? Are you saving for future needs, such as a house, college for the kids, and retirement? What is your net worth?

What does the Summary of Debts reveal? Do you pay all of your credit cards in full every month, or do you have outstanding balances? If you have outstanding credit-card balances,

SAMPLE BALANCE SHEET

Description	Current Year	Prior Year
ASSETS		
Cash and Cash Equivalents		
Cash on Hand	100	100
Cash — Checking	1,100	1,100
Cash — Money Market	—	—
Cash — Other	—	—
Total Cash and Cash Equivalents	1,200	1,200
Invested Assets		
Certificates of Deposit	—	—
Brokerage Accounts	—	—
Retirement Plans	12,000	11,000
Business Investment	—	—
Total Invested Assets	12,000	11,000
Use Assets		
House	250,000	240,000
Autos	15,000	17,000
Other	10,000	10,000
Total Use Assets	275,000	267,000
TOTAL ASSETS	288,200	279,200
LIABILITIES		
Mortgage and Home Equity Loans	200,000	203,000
Auto Loans	10,000	12,000
Credit Cards and Installment Loans	10,000	7,000
Student Loans	—	—
Business Debt	—	—
Other (Loans from Family and Friends; Retirement Plans; Life Insurance)	—	—
TOTAL LIABILITIES	220,000	222,000
NET WORTH	68,200	57,200

SAMPLE SUMMARY OF DEBTS

Type of Debt	To Whom Owed	Balance Due	# of Payments Remaining	Interest Rate	Min Required Monthly Payment	# Months Past Due	Describe What Was Purchased
Mortgage	Name: Home Loan Bank Address: City: State: Zip: Telephone:	200,000	240	5.5%	1,500	—	Home
Total Mortgage/Home Equity		200,000					
Auto	Name: Auto Loan Bank Address: City: State: Zip: Telephone:	10,000	50	8.0%	300	—	Sedan
Total Auto		10,000					
Credit Card	Name: Visa Address: City: State: Zip: Telephone:	4,000	NA	19.0%	120	—	Groceries; medical; misc
Credit Card	Name: Mastercard Address: City: State: Zip: Telephone:	4,000	NA	14.0%	110	—	Misc
Credit Card	Name: Discover Address: City: State: Zip: Telephone:	2,000	NA	17.0%	60	—	Misc
Total Credit Cards/Installment		10,000					

what are the interest rates you are being charged? Are you paying the minimum balance? If you are, be prepared to take many years to pay off your balance. The credit-card companies use formulas that extend payment over many years and cost you a lot of interest. In session four, we'll show you how to eliminate it using the Accelerator Repayment Plan.

HOMEWORK

➤ Complete personal balance sheet and summary of debts.

A THOUGHT FOR THE WEEK

"Pray as if everything depended on God and work as if everything depended on you"

— St. Ignatius Loyola

7 STEPS TO BECOMING FINANCIALLY FREE

STEP ONE   Be a "Steward of Providence"

STEP TWO   Assess Where You Are – Develop a Plan

STEP THREE $2,000 Emergency Savings

STEP FOUR   Eliminate Debt – Accelerate It!

STEP FIVE   Rainy Day Fund – Six Months' Expenses

STEP SIX   Review Insurance and Estate Planning Needs

STEP SEVEN   Save and Invest with a Purpose

CHILDREN AND MONEY
GIVING AND GROWING

PRE-SESSION THREE REQUIREMENTS

➤ Read the following from *7 Steps to Becoming Financially Free*: Chapters 4 and 6.

➤ Complete the following session-three material in the workbook:
   ❏ Review goals for session.
   ❏ Answer discussion topics.
   ❏ Read the letters from Mary Young.
   ❏ Complete reading in practical exercise section.

GOALS — SESSION THREE

➤ Helping your children learn and apply Catholic teaching on handling money in their lives.

➤ Recognize the link that exists between developing a generous attitude and growing in your relationship with the Lord.

➤ Understand the basics of tithing.

➤ Learn how to budget and track your income and expenses.

➤ Develop a regular "financial maintenance" schedule.

OPENING PRAYER AND INTRODUCTORY VIDEO

Led by group leader.

1. **Read the following references:** *Catechism* **2221; Deuteronomy 6:6-7; Proverbs 22:6.**
What is an effective way to teach young children about money? Based upon the reading material in *7 Steps to Becoming Financially Free,* how should you adjust your approach as your children reach the teen years?

_____

_____

_____

_____

_____

_____

2. **Read the following references: Malachi 3:7-10; Matthew 25:35-40; 1 Corinthians 13:3.**
Most often when we think about giving, we are typically concerned with meeting a physical need, whether it's a new Church, school, or missionary work. There are many good reasons to be generous with the resources we have, including helping those who are less fortunate than we are. But what is the *primary* reason we should develop a generous spirit and why is this so?

_____

_____

_____

_____

_____

3. Read the following references: Leviticus 27:30; Proverbs 3:9; Matthew 23:23; 2 Corinthians 9:6-7; St. Irenaeus reading (see Appendix A); *Code of Canon Law* 222 (see Appendix A).

While we have an obligation to support the Church, the amount we choose to give is voluntary. On average, American Catholics give a little over 1% of their income for charitable purposes. The tithe (10%) was the model provided by God in the Old Testament. Is our giving being done as more of an afterthought, and if so, how does that impact our relationship with the Lord?

_____

_____

_____

_____

_____

_____

4. Read the following references: 1 Kings 17:7-16; 2 Kings 4:1-7; Matthew 14:13-21.

It's important that we understand that God is our Father and He loves us with a perfect love. It's up to us to respond to that love in gratitude and trust. How does the act of tithing increase our sense of God's providence in our lives?

_____

_____

_____

_____

_____

5. Read the letters from Mary Young that follow this discussion topic and note how this couple has applied Catholic teaching in the management of their money.

_____

_____

_____

_____

_____

_____

_____

Dear Readers,

The following letters are from a woman (Mary Young is not her real name) who wrote me several years ago. The first letter is brief, but captures the essence of how growing in generosity increases our ability to love.

The second letter does an excellent job of showing how developing and living by a financial plan helps you meet your goals in life. I happen to know that this family lived on a modest income, yet they managed what they had very well. I was so impressed by the example of this family that I wanted to include the letters in these practical exercises. I'm sure that you will not only enjoy them, but profit from them as well. God bless you.

In Christ,

Phil

Dear Mr. Lenahan,

We have learned, sometimes the hard way, that it is perfectly safe to give more than you think you can afford. This is a mystery and I still can't figure it out, but it is true. If you want God to bless your endeavors, help Him bless some other needy organization's endeavors. I don't think this is a "pay back" situation as much as that if we show God that we are trying to learn how to love, He watches over us. Money is both a blessing and a test for all of us, whatever our income is. If we use it selfishly to take care of ourselves only, God must decide that He'll leave us to manage on our own, since we seem to want to. If we can control our fear and our avarice and toss the money where He shows us He wants it, He sees that we trust Him to be our Father and He acts as such in all our endeavors. This is the only explanation I can offer for the fact that, while we have of course been surprised by sudden large expenditures like everyone else, somehow the money has always been there. We have never gone hungry because we helped someone else eat.

In Christ,

Mary Young

Dear Mr. Lenahan,

I was very happy to see a book like yours appear, because in planning a curriculum for our high school students, a major concern has been finding resources to prepare our kids to handle money properly – probably one of life's major tasks. Even Our Lord thought so — look at how often He talks about money in the Gospels!

My husband has had to manage our finances with great care and skill – and a lot of help from above – and this skill has received very little applause from anyone who knows him, because keeping your family out of debt simply is not a priority for most people. My parents, who are very good Catholics, basically always looked to a better job and a higher income to keep them afloat. This meant that my father had to remain in an intense competition to keep climbing the ladder to pay the bills and support the children, and when he finally reached the top, his job was so demanding that he had to almost abandon his family to fill his responsibilities. I remember one evening while we were eating supper, Dad came in carrying his suitcase and briefcase (he had been gone one week on a business trip) and said "Hi, everybody, I'm back home." One of my little brothers looked up in surprise and said," You're back home? I didn't even know you were gone!"

My husband and I are very much alike in many ways: we seldom fight about money because we are both savers, and when there isn't any money we don't spend any. When we were married, we realized that the only way I would be able to stay home on his income would be if we had no mortgage payment. I was teaching at the time, and we decided to live on his income and save as much as we could from that, and save every penny of my income. We bought a small house, paid 3/5 of the asking price in cash, and paid off the rest within 15 months.

Our first child was born nine months later, during the recession of '82-'84, and the next few years were very tight. But because we had no mortgage, we were able to save what used to go into our mortgage payment. Interest rates were high then, and we got a good return on even our small savings. We also saved our income-tax refunds. For years we looked for a bigger house with more property, but because we literally could not afford a mortgage payment, we had to wait until we could save the difference. When we conceived #4 in 1992, we *had* to do something about both the house and the car, but by that time we had managed to save $55,000. We put a $30,000 addition and improvements to the house and bought a new mini-van when there was a big discount at the end of the season.

Our income is low but we have no debts, so we are able to save money to pay cash for what we need. I keep a careful eye on the sales and a have a system of buying ahead what we need instead of waiting until we need it, which requires that I stay organized. My family depends heavily on the work that I do to stretch the money, so in a sense I have a job with a non-taxable income!

Chuck keeps a budget and sets up accounts for each need. He even has a car-repair account in which he sets aside $30 every pay period so that if we need a sudden repair, the money will be there. Why pretend that it won't happen? We stay afloat because we always know exactly where we are in our finances. We've even been able to keep saving, and we already have enough to pay at least one and possibly two university educations. I just love this man and reverence him for the silent, sacrificial, often exhausting work he puts into spinning straw into gold for love of us. And because he loves and trusts God, God does His part, too. There have been so many times when God's providence has saved us money, made something almost broken last just a little longer, made a funny noise in the car disappear…

In contrast, a friend of mine married a man with an excellent salary. They had a large wedding and went to Hawaii for two weeks for their honeymoon. The following year they went to B.C., and then to Quebec, and then to Mexico. She quit work when the baby came, and they bought a lovely ranch on an acre of property near the lake. Now they have a big mortgage, and they argue a lot about money. If they had lived on her small salary and saved every penny of his, they could have paid cash for their home and car and all his income would be theirs to spend now. As it is, they will probably be slaves to the bank for the rest of their lives, and all for the lack of four years of real sacrifice. Young couples don't realize that every penny they spend during their engagement and early marriage is money that will have to be borrowed and paid back at least double over most of their lives when they have to buy a house.

Sincerely in Christ,

Mary Young

P.S. I want to share a prayer with you that we all say every night after the Rosary. It has been miraculous for us and will be for you, too.

> *"O glorious St. Joseph, you who have power to render possible things which are impossible, come to our aid in our present trouble and distress. Take this important and difficult affair under your particular protection, that it may end happily. O dear St. Joseph, all our confidence is in you. Let it not be said that we have invoked you in vain, and since you are so powerful with Jesus and Mary, show that your goodness equals your power. Amen.*
>
> *Divine Providence* can *provide.*
> *Divine Providence* did *provide.*
> *Divine Providence* will *provide."*

The ABC's of Creating a Budget

In the last session, we talked about Step Two of the 7 Steps to Becoming Financially Free, "Assess Where You Are – Develop a Plan." We learned about two important financial planning tools, the balance sheet, and the summary of debts. In this session, we're going to learn about another very important tool, the budget.

You'll recall that I described the balance sheet as a "snapshot" of your financial position at one point in time. The budget, on the other hand, is more like a "video" of your finances over a chosen period of time. A budget is a forecast or projection of what you expect your income and expenses to be during the chosen time frame. Many budget methods focus on a weekly or monthly budget. In my experience, this tends to get people bogged down in details where they have a hard time seeing the forest through the trees. I find an annual budget to be a more effective way to see the big picture.

This practical exercise is broken down into four steps:

- Budget Step A — Complete Guideline Budget Review
- Budget Step B — Create Veritas Annual Budget
- Budget Step C — Track Income and Expenses
- Budget Step D — Complete Periodic Reviews

In preparation for your session-three small-group meeting, I would like you to read through this entire exercise from an overview perspective. It's important that you understand the big picture before you start working through the details. Take some time to review the examples provided for the Stewart family. By understanding how the budgeting information comes together in their case, it will be much easier for you to apply the steps to your circumstances. Once your session is over, you'll come back to these materials and work through the budget steps as part of your homework assignment.

It takes time to get used to the terminology of budgeting and the various "how to's." Don't be intimidated. Take your time and go step by step. While you may start out thinking budgets are constraining, you'll come to see that they are truly liberating, and a key to reaching financial freedom. Once you determine the goals you have for the future, your budget will be one of the key gauges as to whether you are making progress toward meeting those goals.

With the help of the Stewart family, we are going to spend some time now going through the basics of what a budget is and the steps you need to take to develop and maintain one.

Budget Step A — Guideline Budget Review

For many going through this program, the Guideline Budget Review represents a transition from old ways to new ways. It provides an opportunity for a fresh start — one that leads you out of financial bondage to true financial freedom. In this step, you take a look back at where you have been financially. This includes the good, the bad, and the ugly! Some find it hard to take an honest look at where they've been. But don't be afraid. It's the best way for you to move forward on this freedom journey.

Do you remember when you made your first confession? Or do you have a young child who has recently made their first confession? Especially for folks with a sensitive spirit, there is a great deal of trepidation taking that step. But once it is over, there is a joy and peace that comes with having made a good confession. Now don't get me wrong. The Guideline Budget Review isn't confession! But it does involve the same looking back at behavior that may not have been so healthy, and looking ahead to change that behavior based on the Godly principles of financial freedom you have been learning.

With that thought in mind, you'll begin your Guideline Budget Review by estimating your annual income and expenses, and comparing them to the suggested amounts from the Guideline Budget Table. Because very few people have been taught how to use a budget, they often have difficulty determining what amount to allow for each spending category. That is why we provide a guideline budget.

The Guideline Budget Review is only meant to help you get started and show you where you may be overspending. As you continue to track your income and expenses over the next

GUIDELINE BUDGET TABLE — PERCENTAGES						
Gross Income	30,000	45,000	60,000	75,000	90,000	105,000
Tithe/Giving[1]	10%	10%	10%	10%	10%	10%
Taxes[2]	4%	12%	13%	15%	18%	20%
Current Education[3]	–	–	1%	1%	2%	2%
Savings and Investments[4]	5%	5%	7%	9%	9%	10%
Housing	38%	35%	33%	31%	30%	28%
Groceries	13%	12%	11%	11%	9%	9%
Transportation	13%	12%	11%	10%	9%	8%
Medical/Dental	4%	3%	3%	3%	3%	3%
Insurance	4%	3%	3%	3%	3%	3%
Debt Payments	–	–	–	–	–	–
Clothing	3%	2%	2%	2%	2%	2%
Entertainment and Recreation	3%	3%	3%	3%	3%	3%
Work Related	–	–	–	–	–	–
Miscellaneous	3%	3%	3%	2%	2%	2%
Total Spending Percentage	100%	100%	100%	100%	100%	100%

[1] The tithe (10%) is a guideline. Those on low incomes should strive to be generous, but understandably may use more of their resources to meet basic needs. Those with higher incomes may find that 10% is not enough.
[2] Tax percentages are dependent on a number of factors, including the number of children in your family. Review your previous tax returns or consult a tax professional.
[3] Assumes part of tithe used for Catholic school tuition or home-school expenses.
[4] This category includes saving for college and retirement. You should take into account any retirement program benefits from work (401(k); pension) when determining your needs for this category.

few months, you will be in a position to create and update your own personal budget. It will take into account your special circumstances and priorities. It is not important that your spending agree with the guideline in every area, but it is critical that your expenses not exceed your income. Just as important is that your priorities reflect your Catholic faith. Therefore, education, savings, and tithing/giving, are all given high priorities and planned for as any other expense. Take a moment to familiarize yourself with the Guideline Budget Table.

The Guideline Budget Table provides suggested spending for each category as a percentage of gross income. Here are the steps you should take to complete your Guideline Budget Review:

Phase 1 — Determine Income

One of the first steps to take in your Guideline Budget Review is to estimate your annual income. Since the Spending Diary doesn't capture income, you'll need to do a little research to come up with it. Here are a few tips:

- Review last year's tax return for sources and amounts of income, including salary, interest and dividends, income from a business, social security, income associated with your retirement plan, and other sources of income.

- Don't forget to consider irregular sources of income as well, such as commissions, gifts and bonuses.

- Review recent pay stubs to confirm your current salary.

Based on your research, write your income in both the "Estimated Annual Income/Expense" column and the "Guideline Budget" column on your "Guideline Budget Review" form.

In the Stewarts' example, Tom Stewart has a regular salaried position, so it's pretty easy for him to come up with his annual salary. But his company also offers a bonus plan that varies based on the company's results, so he'll have to estimate this when it comes to setting his budget. Tom and Patty's parents also typically make gifts to the family of about $3,000 each year, and they'll want to take these into account when creating their budget. The table below shows how the Stewarts completed the income section of the Guideline Budget Review.

SAMPLE INCOME SECTION				
Account Description	Estimated Annual Income/Expenses	Actual Annual %	Guideline Budget	Guideline Budget %
Gross Income	80,000	100%	80,000	100%
Salary	75,000			
Bonus	2,000			
Interest	—			
Dividends	—			
Retirement Plan	—			
Other	3,000			

Phase 2 — Determine Expenses

Your next step in completing the Guideline Budget Review is to estimate your annual expenses. You've been maintaining your Spending Diary for four weeks. Now you can add up your spending totals by category and have a sense as to how much you are spending each month. By multiplying each of these numbers by 12, you'll have an estimate for what you spend in each category over the course of a year.

Remember that areas where spending doesn't occur evenly over the year, such as Christmas spending, certain insurance bills, property taxes if not part of an impound account, and other irregular expenses won't be accurate. You'll need to adjust these to make them more accurate (see below). But things like entertainment, meals out, groceries, and gas should be reasonably accurate.

Let's look at what the Stewart family's spending diary showed for three categories:

SAMPLE SPENDING DIARY					
Date	Pmt Type	Description	Groceries	Clothing	Entertainment and Recreation
1-Jun	Check	Cox Cable			67
2-Jun	Check	Food Giant-groceries	264		
3-Jun	Credit	Dillards-shoes and socks for kids		62	
3-Jun	Credit	Domino's Pizza-dinner			31
5-Jun	Cash	Crafts Fair-earrings-Patty		22	
5-Jun	Credit	Dan's Drive Up Dairy - Milk	4		
6-Jun	Credit	Walgreens-soda	10		
8-Jun	Credit	Safeway-groceries	192		
11-Jun	Cash	Fred's Fruit Stand-fruit and nuts	15		
12-Jun	Cash	In and Out Burger-lunch			21
12-Jun	Cash	Tubby's Ice Cream Parlor-cones			15
13-Jun	Credit	McDonalds-lunch-kids and friends			27
14-Jun	Credit	Dan's Drive Up Dairy - Milk	4		
16-Jun	Check	Costco-groceries	320		
16-Jun	Check	Costco-swim suit and jeans		55	
16-Jun	Credit	Nordstrom - Anniversary outfit		194	
19-Jun	Credit	Domino's Pizza-dinner			33
20-Jun	Credit	Kiss's Fine Dining-anniv. dinner			58
21-Jun	Credit	Dan's Drive Up Dairy - Milk	4		
23-Jun	Credit	Food Giant-groceries	42		
26-Jun	Check	Food Giant-groceries	17		
26-Jun	Cash	Tubby's Ice Cream Parlor-cones			15
28-Jun	Credit	Safeway-groceries	61		
Monthly Total			933	333	267
Estimated Annual Expense (Multiply by 12)			11,200	4,000	3,200

7 STEPS TO BECOMING FINANCIALLY FREE WORKBOOK

SESSION THREE

As I mentioned above, some spending categories don't occur evenly through the year. As a result, you'll need to do a little research to get a handle on those expenses. Review your checkbook register, bank and credit-card statements, tax return and receipts for expenses you don't feel the spending diary properly captured. This may include such items as tuition, insurance, property taxes, home improvements, car repairs, medical bills, and holiday spending. Total your annual irregular expenses by subcategory on the Guideline Budget Review form.

One of the Stewart family's irregular expenses is their annual vacation. They expect to spend $1,000 this year. In the table below, you can see how the Stewarts' budget includes annual estimates for the expenses from their spending diary as well as their estimate of vacation costs.

SAMPLE EXPENSE ESTIMATES SECTION				
Account Description	Estimated Annual Income/Expenses	Actual Annual %	Guideline Budget	Guideline Budget %
Groceries	11,200			
Clothing	4,000			
Entertain. and Recreation	4,200			
Eating Out	2,400			
Babysitting	—			
Cable/Satellite/Movies	800			
Allowances	—			
Activities	—			
Vacation	1,000			

This brings us to our next step:

Phase 3 — Complete Expense Section of Guideline Budget Review

- Using your Spending Diary and the other information you have gathered, estimate your annual spending. Do this as best you can based on the sub-categories provided. I understand that your Spending Diary only captured the information by main category. But by reviewing who you paid and the brief descriptions you listed, you should be able to provide amounts at the sub-category level. Doing this will provide you valuable information as you begin to develop your future plans. Write the amounts on the appropriate line under the estimated annual amount column.

- Add the estimated annual amounts listed in each sub-category and write the total on the main category line. For example, the Stewarts estimate they'll spend $1,500 on doctor bills, $500 at the dentist, and $400 on prescriptions. These add up to $2,400, which is the total the Stewarts show for the Medical Expenses main category.

- Divide the estimated annual amount for each main category by your total estimated gross income (before taxes) and write the percentage in the estimated annual percentage column. For example, in the Stewarts' sample that follows, Housing and Home Expenses total $30,400; $30,400 divided by the gross income of $80,000 equals 38%.

- Go back to the Guideline Budget Table at the beginning of this practical exercise and find the column that most closely approximates your annual income. Use the percentages from that column for each spending category. For example, if your gross income is $80,000, like the Stewart family, you'll use the percentages from the $75,000 column, since it is closest to $80,000. The guideline budget % for groceries in the $75,000 column is 11%. Write the percentages onto your Guideline Budget Review form in the "Guideline Budget %" column.

- Multiply the % in each spending category in the "Guideline Budget %" column by the Gross Income amount you listed in the "Guideline Budget" column. This will provide a guideline spending amount by main category. For example, the transportation guideline % for the Stewarts is 10%. Based on their annual gross income of $80,000, their annual guideline budget equals $8,000.

- The bottom of the form includes a section summarizing your total income and expenses. Complete this summary. When your income exceeds your expenses, this is shown by a positive amount; if your expenses exceed your income, it is shown by a negative amount or in parenthesis.

- Notice that in addition to showing dollars, the budget looks at spending by each main category as a percentage of gross income. This is a common way of analyzing financial information. It will help you better understand where your money is going.

Let's Look at the Stewarts' Personal Guideline Budget Review

Tom and Patty Stewart are in their late thirties and have four children ranging from 1 to 14 years of age. Tom has a good job as a middle manager of a small manufacturing company, and Patty is a full-time homemaker. They have never really learned how to manage their money, and they have never established any specific financial goals.

They have basically lived month to month, and when there was a little too much month left at the end of the money, they relied on credit cards to get them through. Their oldest child is reaching college age, and they don't have a plan to assist with college expenses. They realize that they aren't getting any younger and that they need to look toward providing for their retirement. With all this in mind, let's take a look at the Stewarts' Guideline Budget Review:

You can see that the Stewart family is estimating that their annual expenses exceed their income by $4,500, or 6% of their income. By comparing the actual percentages to the guideline budget percentages, we can determine which areas are most out of line and should be looked into. For the Stewarts, the most significant differences show up in the categories of tithe/giving, savings, housing, savings, and debt payments along with other lesser categories.

SAMPLE GUIDELINE BUDGET REVIEW

Account Description	Estimated Annual Income/Expenses	Actual Annual %	Guideline Budget	Guideline Budget %
Gross Income	80,000	100%	80,000	100%
Salary	75,000			
Bonus	2,000			
Interest	—			
Dividends	—			
Retirement Plan	—			
Other	3,000			
Tithe/Giving	800	1%	8,000	10%
Deductible	800			
Non-deductible	—			
Children Tuition	—			
Taxes	13,600	17%	12,000	15%
Federal Income	5,000			
State Income	2,000			
Social Security	5,000			
Medicare	1,200			
State Disability	400			
Current Education	200	0%	800	1%
Tuition (See tithe)	—			
Supplies	200			
Day Care	—			
Other	—			
Savings	—	0%	7,200	9%
Emergency and Rainy Day	—			
Future Education	—			
Retirement Plan	—			
Housing and Home Expenses	30,400	38%	24,800	31%
Mortgage/rent	18,000			
Insurance	800			
Taxes	3,000			
Electricity	1,000			
Gas	900			
Water	800			
Gardening	800			
Housecleaning	—			
Telephone	1,000			
Maintenance	1,500			
Pest Control	400			
Association Dues	—			
Bottled Water	—			
Postage	200			
Miscellaneous	—			
Improvements	2,000			
Groceries	11,200	14%	8,800	11%

continued on next page...

SAMPLE GUIDELINE BUDGET REVIEW (continued from page 39)

Account Description	Estimated Annual Income/Expenses	Actual Annual %	Guideline Budget	Guideline Budget %
Transportation	7,700	10%	8,000	10%
Payment/Replace Savings	3,600			
Gas/Oil	2,000			
Insurance	800			
License/Taxes	300			
Maintenance/Repair	1,000			
Medical Expenses	2,400	3%	2,400	3%
Doctor	1,500			
Dentist	500			
Prescriptions	400			
Other	—			
Insurance	2,400	3%	2,400	3%
Medical	900			
Life	1,500			
Disability	—			
Debt Payments	3,500	4%	—	0%
Credit Card	3,500			
Loans and Notes	—			
Other	—			
Clothing	4,000	5%	1,600	2%
Entertain. and Recreation	5,100	6%	2,400	3%
Eating Out	3,300			
Babysitting	—			
Cable/Satellite/Movies	800			
Allowances	—			
Activities	—			
Vacation	1,000			
Work Related	—	0%	—	0%
Education/Dues	—			
Internet/Phone	—			
Other	—			
Miscellaneous	3,200	4%	1,600	2%
Beauty/Barber/Cosmetics	800			
Laundry	200			
Subscriptions	200			
Holiday/Gifts	1,700			
Accounting/Legal	100			
Veterinarian/Animals	200			
Summary of Inc./Exp.				
Total Income	80,000	100%	80,000	100%
Total Expenses	84,500	106%	80,000	100%
Income Over/(Under) Exp.	(4,500)	-6%	—	0%

Budget Step B — Create Your Veritas Annual Budget

Your First "Family Budget" Meeting

At this point, it becomes possible to make some initial decisions about spending priorities. As I wrote at the beginning of this exercise, this is where you take a look back at where you have been, and make an open and honest assessment. It's where you begin to review your priorities with the understanding that the Lord wants you to be a Steward of Providence. He has entrusted His resources for you to manage in ways that are pleasing to Him. What an awesome responsibility!

For husbands and wives going through this program, this is an important time. You'll want to make sure there is open and respectful communication between the two of you. It's not a time to be critical or judgmental about the past, but to move forward with a Godly, prayerful perspective. The Stewarts decided to get a baby-sitter for a few hours so they could go to a quiet place and talk about their family's financial priorities. After discussing their Guideline Budget Review, Tom and Patty have decided to make the following initial adjustments:

- After reading the Bible and *Catechism* references related to generosity, they have developed a desire to increase their giving. They will do so in increments with the goal of increasing their giving from $800 per year to $3,500.

- The Stewarts have decided to provide a Catholic education for their children. In doing so, they recognize that the Catholic tuition can be part of their tithe. Moving the tuition costs to the tithe category brings their overall giving to 8%, which is a great start on the tithing journey!

- As a result of their tithing decision, they now have increased deductions for tax purposes, resulting in a lower tax liability.

- Savings has been increased to $1,000 in order to fully fund the $2,000 Emergency Fund by the end of the year (the Stewarts already had $1,000 in emergency reserves). In addition, Tom is now taking advantage of the 2% match that his company offers through its 401K plan. The Stewarts will emphasize saving more once their consumer credit is eliminated.

- The Stewarts have committed to using the Accelerator Repayment Plan to eliminate their consumer credit, including their auto loan (will cover in session four). They have agreed to use credit cards in the future only if they pay the current month's purchases in full. Otherwise, they will cut the cards up and cancel them. They have committed to paying $800 per month, or $9,600 per year for debt repayments. This $9,600 is being allocated this year as follows: $1,000 to fully fund the $2,000 Emergency Fund; $3,600 continuing payments on their auto loan; the remaining $5,000 will be used to pay down their credit-card debt.

- The Stewarts had hired a gardener a year before, and they decided to go back to doing the yard work themselves for $600 in savings in the housing category. They also reduced their spending on improvements by $1,000, along with other more modest adjustments.

- In the groceries category, the Stewarts realized they were purchasing a lot of prepackaged foods, which added significantly to their spending. By reducing the amount of convenience foods and cooking more from scratch, they were able to reduce spending in this category by $2,400.

- The Stewarts had been shopping for clothing as a recreational pursuit at the trendier department stores. They realize they can reduce expenses if they shop sales carefully and focus more on handing down clothes for the younger children, rather than always buying new. They believe they can save $2,400.

- In the area of entertainment and recreation, the Stewarts realize they need to cut back on eating out, which has become a weekly event. They will also eliminate the cable television. Instead of expensive outings, they will work on planning less costly family activities, such as picnics, camping, etc. They estimate reducing spending in this area by $3,000.

- In the miscellaneous category, the Stewarts agreed to begin cutting the hair of the youngest children themselves, eliminate their subscriptions, using the library instead, and reduce their holiday spending by $500. Total estimated savings amount to $1,100.

Once you have your first "Family Budget Meeting" and see where you have been, you'll probably find that you want to make some adjustments to better reflect your life's true goals, just like the Stewarts.

Your Guideline Budget Review was a one-time effort. From this point on, you'll use the Veritas Budget Worksheet. Once you've decided on your new spending priorities, update the annual budget section of the Veritas Budget Worksheet. Then, as you track your income and expenses through the year (Budget Step C), this form will summarize that information for you. You'll easily be able to compare your actual income and spending to your budgeted amounts to make sure your plan is on track. Remember to visit www.VeritasFinancialMinistries.com to see if the online budgeting system works for you.

You can see on the next page how the Stewarts incorporated into their Veritas Budget the changes they had discussed during their Guideline Budget Review.

Budget Step C — Track Income and Expenses

Now that you have created your Veritas Budget, it's important that you continue to track your income and expenses so you can see if you are following your plan. Let's talk about the different ways this can be done.

Tracking Income and Expenses

You have been using the Spending Diary to record your expenses for the last several weeks. We've had you use this simple method so you get used to the idea of tracking your spending. Now it's time to move to a more formal system for tracking your income and expenses. You have a number of options. Computer-based programs are getting easier to use and take much of the drudgery out of this step. One of those options is the online budgeting program at www.VeritasFinancialMinistries.com. This program will be especially useful if you like the reports

SAMPLE VERITAS BUDGET WORKSHEET

Account Description	Year-to-date Income/Expenses	Actual Annual %	Annual Budget	Annual Budget %
Gross Income			81,500	100%
Salary			75,000	
Bonus			2,000	
Interest			—	
Dividends			—	
Retirement Plan			1,500	
Other			3,000	
Tithe/Giving			6,500	8%
Deductible			3,500	
Non-deductible				
Children Tuition			3,000	
Taxes			12,100	15%
Federal Income			4,000	
State Income			1,500	
Social Security			5,000	
Medicare			1,200	
State Disability			400	
Current Education			—	0%
Tuition (See tithe)				
Supplies				
Day Care				
Other				
Savings			4,000	5%
Emergency and Rainy Day			1,000	
Future Education				
Retirement Plan			3,000	
Housing and Home Expenses			27,400	34%
Mortgage/rent			18,000	
Insurance			800	
Taxes			3,000	
Electricity			800	
Gas			800	
Water			700	
Gardening			200	
Housecleaning			—	
Telephone			800	
Maintenance			1,000	
Pest Control			200	
Association Dues			—	
Bottled Water			—	
Postage			100	
Miscellaneous			—	
Improvements			1,000	
Groceries			8,800	11%

continued on next page...

CHILDREN AND MONEY; GIVING AND GROWING

SAMPLE VERITAS BUDGET WORKSHEET (continued from page 43)

Account Description	Year-to-date Income/Expenses	Actual Annual %	Annual Budget	Annual Budget %
Transportation			7,100	9%
Payment/Replace Savings			3,600	
Gas/Oil			1,500	
Insurance			700	
License/Taxes			300	
Maintenance/Repair			1,000	
Medical Expenses			2,400	3%
Doctor			1,500	
Dentist			500	
Prescriptions			400	
Other				
Insurance			2,400	3%
Medical			900	
Life			1,500	
Disability				
Debt Payments			5,000	6%
Credit Card			5,000	
Loans and Notes				
Other				
Clothing			1,600	2%
Entertain. and Recreation			2,100	3%
Eating Out			600	
Babysitting			—	
Cable/Satellite/Movies			—	
Allowances			200	
Activities			400	
Vacation			900	
Work Related			—	0%
Education/Dues			—	
Internet/Phone			—	
Other			—	
Miscellaneous			2,100	3%
Beauty/Barber/Cosmetics			500	
Laundry			100	
Subscriptions			—	
Holiday/Gifts			1,200	
Accounting/Legal			100	
Veterinarian/Animals			200	
Summary of Inc./Exp.				
Total Income			81,500	100%
Total Expenses			81,500	100%
Income Over/(Under) Exp.			—	0%

used in this study, including the Spending Diary, Balance Sheet, Summary of Debts, Guideline Budget Review, and the Veritas Budget. You can also use one of the nationally known programs.

If you prefer a manual system, you can use the Veritas paper forms or an envelope-based system. Some people like to combine an envelope system with a computer-based system. Before we go further, I need to review how you get your spending information from your checkbook to your budget.

Checkbook Register

The checkbook register is the original source for the actual expenses that you see on the budget worksheet. This is where all of your checks, automatic teller machine and debit card withdrawals, deposits, and other banking activities are documented. But the information isn't organized in a way that lets you see how you are progressing according to your plan. That's where the individual account register comes in.

Individual Account Register

The Individual Account Register is used to summarize your checkbook activity by the categories used on the budget worksheet. A separate account sheet is used for each sub-category that applies to your situation. The form has columns for the date, check number, description, amount, and cumulative total. The amount in the cumulative total column is what periodically gets transferred to the budget worksheet. I have found that using a cumulative total throughout the year, rather than looking at each month separately, provides the most accurate picture of a family's income and expenses.

CHECK REGISTER

Date	Payment Type	Number	Description	Deposit Amount	Payment Amount	Balance
1/1/xx		Deposit	Tom's Paycheck	3,000.00		3,000.00
1/1/xx	Check	101	Marty's Auto Repair		132.57	1,867.43
1/5/xx	Check	102	Super Grocery Store		83.42	1,784.01
1/7/xx	Debit	NA	Drive-Thru Dairy		18.64	1,765.37

INDIVIDUAL ACCOUNT REGISTER

Account Description: Groceries				
Date	Payment Type/#	Description	Amount	Cumulative Total
1/5/xx	Check–102	Super Grocery Store	83.42	83.42
1/7/xx	Debit–NA	Drive-Thru Dairy	18.64	102.06

Tracking by Sub Categories

In order to start you out in baby steps, we had you record your spending on the Spending Diary according to the main categories we use on the Veritas Budget Worksheet. While this information is good, you'll want to have better information available when examining your spending priorities. That's why the Veritas Budget Worksheet uses sub-categories in addition to the main categories. For example, the main category, Entertainment and Recreation, includes the following sub-categories:

- Eating Out
- Baby Sitting
- Cable/Satellite/Movies
- Allowances
- Activities
- Vacation

As you saw on the Stewarts' original Spending Diary, they spent $267 in the Entertainment and Recreation main category. However, $67 was spent in the Cable sub-category, and $200 was spent on Eating Out. Knowing this helps the Stewarts better understand their spending behavior, which is important if they want to reach their goals. From here on out, you'll want to track your income and expenses by the sub-categories on the budget worksheet.

The Cash and Envelope System

When you pay for an item with a check, debit card, or credit card, you end up with a record of your purchase. When you pay cash for an item, unless you keep your receipt, there will be no record of your purchase. Learning how to manage and track your cash spending, especially if you do a lot of it, is a very important part of good budgeting.

A system that has been used for many years (long before computers were invented) is the envelope system. While it's not my preference that the envelope system be used as the entire budgeting method, envelopes can be a big help for heavy cash spending categories. Most often this includes groceries, eating out, or other forms of entertainment and recreation.

If you use cash for any of the sub-categories on the Veritas Budget Worksheet, create an envelope for each one you use. Each month, or pay period, whichever works better for you, you'll withdraw cash equal to your budgeted spending for that time frame for each of the categories. When you withdraw the cash, make sure you note how much you are allocating to each envelope (category) on your checkbook register. This will be the amount you transfer to your Individual Account Register. Then, place the appropriate amount of cash in each of the envelopes. You then spend from the envelope, placing receipts in the envelope in order to have a short-term record. When there is no cash left in the envelope, you don't spend on that category until your next scheduled time to make a cash withdrawal at the bank.

Tracking Expenses and the Individual Account Register — Let's Visit the Stewart Family

The Stewarts were given the assignment to begin tracking their expenses using the Individual Account Registers. Remember, they had completed their Veritas Budget Worksheet after doing their Guideline Budget Review. By tracking their income and expenses, they can verify that their estimates were accurate and keep their plan on track.

The Stewarts have income from Mr. Stewart's job in the form of both salary and bonus. Tom's company also offers a 401K plan with a matching fund up to 2% of salary. Tom and Patty also have other income in the form of gifts from their parents. Therefore, they have four separate Individual Account Registers for income. The same concept applies for the spending categories. Under the automobile category, the Stewarts show expenses for car payments, gas and oil, insurance, licenses, and maintenance. Therefore, they used five Individual Account Registers to track spending in the Transportation category.

The examples below show the Individual Account Registers for Tom's salary and for gas and oil, insurance, and maintenance on the cars for the first three months of the year. The examples on page 48 and 49 show how this information has been transferred to the Veritas Budget Worksheet.

SAMPLE INDIVIDUAL ACCOUNT REGISTERS

Account Description: Salary

Date	Check #	Description	Amount	Cumulative Total
1-Jan	6362	ABC Manufacturing	6,250	6,250.00
1-Feb	6406	ABC Manufacturing	6,250	12,500.00
1-Mar	6449	ABC Manufacturing	6,250	18,750.00

Account Description: Gas/Oil

Date	Check #	Description	Amount	Cumulative Total
1-Jan	1023	Visa	125	125.00
1-Feb	1063	Visa	150	275.00
1-Mar	1093	Visa	100	375.00

Account Description: Auto Insurance

Date	Check #	Description	Amount	Cumulative Total
1-Feb	1063	Expensive Auto Insurance Co	175	175.00

Account Description: Auto Maintenance

Date	Check #	Description	Amount	Cumulative Total
15-Jan	1075	Discover	50	50.00
20-Feb	1080	Discover	75	125.00

Budget Step D — Periodic Review

This final step in the budgeting process is where you periodically compare your actual income and spending to your budgeted amounts on the Veritas Budget Worksheet. Once you fully implement your tracking system (Step C), you'll have this information at your fingertips.

SAMPLE VERITAS BUDGET WORKSHEET

Account Description	Year-to-date Income/Expenses	Actual Annual %	Annual Budget	Annual Budget %
Gross Income	20,375	100%	81,500	100%
Salary	18,750		75,000	
Bonus	500		2,000	
Interest	—		—	
Dividends	—		—	
Retirement Plan	375		1,500	
Other	750		3,000	
Tithe/Giving	1,625	8%	6,500	8%
Deductible	875		3,500	
Non-deductible	—			
Children Tuition	750		3,000	
Taxes	3,025	15%	12,100	15%
Federal Income	1,000		4,000	
State Income	375		1,500	
Social Security	1,250		5,000	
Medicare	300		1,200	
State Disability	100		400	
Current Education	—	0%	—	0%
Tuition (See tithe)	—			
Supplies	—			
Day Care	—			
Other	—			
Savings	1,000	5%	4,000	5%
Emergency and Rainy Day	250		1,000	
Future Education	—			
Retirement Plan	750		3,000	
Housing and Home Expenses	6,775	33%	27,400	34%
Mortgage/rent	4,500		18,000	
Insurance	200		800	
Taxes	750		3,000	
Electricity	200		800	
Gas	200		800	
Water	180		700	
Gardening	20		200	
Housecleaning	—		—	
Telephone	200		800	
Maintenance	250		1,000	
Pest Control	50		200	
Association Dues	—		—	
Bottled Water	—		—	
Postage	25		100	
Miscellaneous	—		—	
Improvements	200		1,000	
Groceries	2,200	11%	8,800	11%

continued on next page...

7 STEPS TO BECOMING FINANCIALLY FREE WORKBOOK

SAMPLE VERITAS BUDGET WORKSHEET (continued from page 48)

Account Description	Year-to-date Income/Expenses	Actual Annual %	Annual Budget	Annual Budget %
Transportation	1,650	8%	6,600	8%
Payment/Replace Savings	900		3,600	
Gas/Oil	375		1,500	
Insurance	175		700	
License/Taxes	75		300	
Maintenance/Repair	125		500	
Medical Expenses	575	3%	2,400	3%
Doctor	350		1,500	
Dentist	125		500	
Prescriptions	100		400	
Other	—			
Insurance	550	3%	2,400	3%
Medical	200		900	
Life	350		1,500	
Disability	—			
Debt Payments	1,500	7%	6,000	7%
Credit Card	1,500		6,000	
Loans and Notes	—			
Other	—			
Clothing	250	1%	1,000	1%
Entertain. and Recreation	310	2%	2,150	3%
Eating Out	150		600	
Babysitting	—		—	
Cable/Satellite/Movies	—		—	
Allowances	60		250	
Activities	100		400	
Vacation	—		900	
Work Related	—	0%	—	0%
Education/Dues	—		—	
Internet/Phone	—		—	
Other	—		—	
Miscellaneous	315	2%	2,150	3%
Beauty/Barber/Cosmetics	125		500	
Laundry	25		100	
Subscriptions	15		50	
Holiday/Gifts	100		1,200	
Accounting/Legal	—		100	
Veterinarian/Animals	50		200	
Summary of Inc./Exp.				
Total Income	20,375	100%	81,500	100%
Total Expenses	19,775	97%	81,500	100%
Income Over/(Under) Exp.	600	3%	—	0%

During this review, you'll compare year-to-date spending by category to your annual budget, both in dollars and as percentages of gross income. You'll initially want to focus on how the actual percentages compare to your budgeted percentages. This is because your budgeted dollars are for the whole year, while your actual dollars are year-to-date, which makes comparing actual and budgeted dollars a little like comparing apples and oranges. If you have categories where the actual and budget percentages are different, you'll want to look at the dollar activity that is part of that category to see what the causes are. You can then take corrective action if necessary.

Receiving solid counsel is an important part of these periodic reviews. If you are single, seek the guidance of a Godly mentor who you can touch base with as you complete your review. You'll gain confidence that you have a solid plan, and that you are managing your resources in ways consistent with your call to be a Steward of Providence. If you are married, this counsel should be provided by your spouse, however, the two of you may also benefit from the help of a Godly friend. The Family Budget Meetings are designed to help you with these periodic reviews. It's a time for you to review your goals, share concerns about how the plan is unfolding, and make adjustments to the plan based on life events. Take advantage of them!

One of the keys to succeeding with your financial plan is to get and stay organized. I'd like to share a few tips both now and in session four about how you can get more financially organized.

Develop a Regular "Maintenance" Schedule

When I visit with counselees, I can often see by their glazed eyes that they were up late the night before finishing their paperwork in preparation for our meeting. Rather than having the financial planning process be a fire drill each month, I encourage you to take time each week to pay bills and record your expenses. I have found that by taking just an additional hour each week, you can avoid that big buildup of paperwork that is so depressing to deal with. I strongly urge you to establish a fixed time each week to pay bills, update your checkbook, and track your expenses.

When you sit down to pay your bills and update your financial information, make sure you have all of the supplies you will need such as your checkbook, envelopes, a pen, postage stamps, return-address stamp, and calculator. Retrieve all of your bills to pay from your "open bills" file. Review them for accuracy and prioritize them for payment. If not due until after your next bill-paying session (including sufficient mailing time), place them back in the open bills file.

Write the checks (don't forget to sign them!), place in the envelopes, stamp and mail. Document your expenditures in your check register and update the appropriate Individual Account Register. Mark the checkbook register with a special checkmark to note that the amount has been transferred to your Individual Account Register.

Now It's Your Turn — You Can Do It Too!

I want you to take your homework assignment this week in steps as follows:

- Complete your Guideline Budget Review. Follow the instructions for phases 1-3 as outlined in Step A of the budgeting process.
- Hold your first "Family Budget Meeting." Consider the following questions to get you thinking about your priorities. Consider the information in light of the 7 Steps to Becoming Financially Free:
  - Does the summary at the bottom of your Guideline Budget Review show you are living within your means (income exceeds expenses), or are you spending more than you earn?
  - How do your spending percentages compare to the guideline budget spending percentages for each of the main categories? Do your spending habits reflect your being a "Steward of Providence," especially when it comes to charitable giving, educating your children, and saving for future needs?
  - Do your spending patterns show that you are getting caught up in the consumer culture?
  - What initial spending adjustments do you anticipate making?
  - If you have consumer debt, consider how much you can allocate toward repaying those debts by using the Accelerator Repayment Plan discussed further in session four.
  - Set a regular schedule for your future "Family Budget Meetings." For those just starting out, you'll want to have these at least monthly, maybe even weekly. For those that are more advanced, quarterly should be adequate, although it may take a few years to reach that point.
- Create your first Veritas Budget.
- Choose the budgeting method that you will use from here on out (Veritas online; other computer program; envelope system; Veritas paper method) and begin the process of tracking your income and expenses.

If you have questions, refer to the example of the Stewart family, ask your group leader, or visit the Veritas web site at www.VeritasFinancialMinistries.com for more information. As you continue developing your plan, keep in mind the 7 Steps to Becoming Financially Free. Remember that it will take several months to develop your budgeting skills. You'll discover expenses coming out of the woodwork that you just didn't consider in your Guideline Budget Review that need to be factored in. After three months of tracking, you'll want to complete a revised budget where you refine the information based on your actual experiences during the tracking period. Use this opportunity to adjust behavior patterns once again in order to bring your spending in line with your plan.

Don't be afraid of the budget. It's a lot like learning to ride a bike. Once you get it, the principles will stick with you for a lifetime. It really is a key to becoming financially free. Remember, when you know where your money is going, you can choose where you want it to go, instead of wondering where it all went! God bless you.

➤ Complete your Guideline Budget Review.

➤ Hold your first "Family Budget Meeting."

➤ Create your Veritas Budget.

➤ Choose the method of budgeting and tracking of income and expenses you will use and get started.

➤ Establish your "financial maintenance" schedule.

A THOUGHT FOR THE WEEK

Serva ordinem, et ordo servabit te,
which means, "Serve order and order will serve you."

7 STEPS TO BECOMING FINANCIALLY FREE

 STEP ONE Be a "Steward of Providence"

 STEP TWO Assess Where You Are – Develop a Plan

 STEP THREE $2,000 Emergency Savings

 STEP FOUR Eliminate Debt – Accelerate It!

 STEP FIVE Rainy Day Fund – Six Months' Expenses

 STEP SIX Review Insurance and Estate Planning Needs

 STEP SEVEN Save and Invest with a Purpose

7 STEPS TO BECOMING FINANCIALLY FREE
BREAKING FREE FROM DEBT

PRE-SESSION FOUR REQUIREMENTS

➤ Read the following from *7 Steps to Becoming Financially Free*: Chapters 7 and 8.

➤ Complete the following session-four material in the workbook:
  ❏ Review goals for session.
  ❏ Answer discussion topics.
  ❏ Complete reading in practical exercise section.

GOALS — SESSION FOUR

➤ Review the 7 Steps to Becoming Financially Free.

➤ Understand the different types of debt available today and the limited circumstances it may make sense to make use of debt.

➤ Recognize why it's important to eliminate all of your consumer debt, and develop a plan to do so using the Accelerator Repayment Plan.

➤ Create your filing system.

OPENING PRAYER AND INTRODUCTORY VIDEO

Led by group leader.

1. The first step to becoming financially free is becoming a "Steward of Providence." Why is this the most important step?

_____

_____

_____

_____

_____

2. **Read Luke 14:28-30.**

The second step to becoming financially free is to assess where you are and develop a plan. Many people try to use their checkbook as the source for making financial decisions, but it doesn't really provide the information needed. How does a budget help you move forward in the seven-step process? How does the guideline budget help with that effort?

_____

_____

_____

_____

_____

3. Discuss the importance of tracking your income and expenses throughout the year. Consider the merits and drawbacks of each of the budgeting methods (envelope; Veritas paper-based; Veritas internet-based; National brand computer programs).

_____

_____

_____

_____

_____

_____

4. **Read the following references: Deuteronomy 15:5-6; Proverbs 22:7; 22:26-27; 6:1-5; Habakkuk 2:6-7; *Catechism* 2410-2411.**
What caution does the Bible and *Catechism* suggest when it comes to going into debt?

_____

_____

_____

_____

_____

5. How can you determine whether you can safely use credit cards? What rule of thumb should you use in determining whether you use debt to make a purchase?

_____

_____

_____

_____

_____

_____

6. How can you develop a plan to overcome any consumer debt that you have accumulated?

_____

_____

_____

_____

_____

7. **Read 1 Timothy 5:8; Proverbs 13:22; 20:21.**

Why is it so important for insurance and estate planning needs to be considered once you have children?

_____

_____

_____

_____

_____

_____

*T*he practical exercises this week are focused on eliminating your debt and beginning to formally track your expenses for your new budget. Before we learn more about the Accelerator Repayment Plan, let's review the need for the initial $2,000 emergency fund.

Emergency Fund

Step Three in the 7 Steps to Becoming Financially Free is to establish an initial emergency savings fund of $2,000. This will also be the beginning of your rainy-day fund in Step Five, but it's important that you establish an initial fund even before you begin paying down your debts in Step Four. Otherwise, you'll find that "Murphy's Law" strikes, and you'll be confronted with "surprise" expenses that will force you to add to your existing credit card balances. The $2,000 emergency fund helps you break the debt cycle. Where should you keep your initial emergency fund? I suggest you put it in a separate money market fund or account. You can earn interest and the money will be there when you need it. If you have to tap into the account, make sure you replenish it as soon as possible. That will probably mean suspending your Accelerator Repayment Plan until you've brought the account back to its $2,000 balance.

Applying the Accelerator Repayment Plan to the Stewart Family Debts

The Stewart family's Summary of Debts has been reprinted below. As you can see, it includes their mortgage, a car loan, and three credit-card balances. For purposes of this exercise, we are going to focus on repaying the outstanding consumer credit, which includes the three credit cards and the car loan. We'll look at the mortgage in the next exercise.

STEWART FAMILY SUMMARY OF DEBTS				
Owed To	Balance	Rate	Payments Remaining	Minimum Payment
House Loan	200,000	6%	360	1,200
Car Loan	10,000	8%	50	300
Visa	4,000	19%	NA	120
Mastercard	4,000	14%	NA	110
Discover	2,000	17%	NA	60

Here is the way I explained how the Accelerator Repayment Plan works in *7 Steps to Becoming Financially Free*:

"The Accelerator Repayment Plan is a simple and straightforward approach to eliminating your consumer credit as rapidly as possible. How fast you eliminate your debt will partly depend on your circumstances, but it will also depend on how motivated you are to get out of debt and how committed you are to making the plan work.

"Let's consider the example of Tom and Patty, who have three credit cards with balances totaling $10,000 and a car loan for $10,000. Their information is presented in the table below. The minimum monthly payments total $590. If they continue to make the minimum payments, it would take them about four years to become debt free, but Tom and Patty would like to be debt free more quickly. After reviewing their budget, they have determined that they will allocate $800 each month for debt repayment. Rather than repaying the debts in four years, this plan eliminates them in less than two and a half years, and will save a bundle in interest charges. Let's review the seven steps that make up the Accelerator Repayment Plan:

1. Make a commitment to go no further into debt. If you can't muster the discipline to avoid purchases that you can't pay off immediately, cut your credit cards up.

2. Make sure that you have your $2,000 emergency fund set aside so that you'll be able to hold to your commitment when "surprises" occur.

3. Develop a realistic budget that includes a monthly amount dedicated to debt repayments. Your budget should balance after taking this monthly payment into account. As you're developing this plan to determine how much you can allocate to debt repayment, use the Accelerator Repayment Plan calculator at www.VeritasFinancialMinistries.com to consider different scenarios. As long as you know how much you owe and the average interest rate, you can play "what if" scenarios to see how long it would take to be debt free at different payment levels.

4. The Accelerator Repayment Plan requires that you prioritize your debts for repayment. My preference, and the one that saves the most money, is to list your debts in order based on interest rate, with the highest rate debt listed first. Some people prefer to list the smallest debt first. They receive encouragement when the smaller credit card balances and monthly statements go away relatively quickly. Choose the method that will work best for you.

ACCELERATOR REPAYMENT PLAN EXAMPLE — TOM AND PATTY'S DEBTS					
Owed To	Balance	Monthly Rate	Minimum Payment	# Payments Based on Minimum Payment	# Payments Based on Accelerator Plan (a)
Visa	4,000	19%	120	48	14 payments at $330
Discover	2,000	17%	60	46	14 payments at $60 and 4 payments at $390
MasterCard	4,000	14%	110	48	18 payments at $110 and 6 payments at $500
Car Loan	10,000	8%	300	38	24 payments at $300 and 5 payments at $800
Totals	20,000	NA	590	NA	NA

Every month you'll make the minimum payment required on each of the loans, except for the loan at the top of the repayment list. This is the one you're accelerating. In the example above, the minimum payment on the Visa bill is $120, but because Tom and Patty have committed $800 per month ($210 more than the minimum payment required on all loans), they can apply the additional $210 each month to the Visa card, for a total of $330. When the Visa bill is paid off, they'll continue applying $800 each month to the outstanding debts. With the Visa bill gone, they can zero in on the Discover Card. By adding the $330 payment they were making on the Visa to the $60 minimum payment they're making on the Discover Card, they have a new payment of $390. You can see how that amount will pay off the Discover Card in no time. You just repeat this process until the debts are eliminated!

5. You can reduce the time it will take to be debt-free even further by being creative about coming up with additional funds that can be applied to the Accelerator Repayment Plan. Consider having a garage sale or taking a temporary second job until the debts are eliminated. The plan will move as fast as you're committed to it moving.

6. Be accountable to someone. This can be your spouse, but if you don't have the discipline to stick with the plan on your own, bring in a friend, family member, or pastor to help you stay on track.

7. Set up a visual system to show your progress, such as a chart on the refrigerator that shows your declining debt balances. Depending on the circumstances, it's not uncommon for a debt repayment plan to take from one to five years, so a visual aid that tracks your progress can help you persevere.

"Once you're debt-free, think of the freedom of having $800 (or whatever amount you had allocated toward your debt) available each month for other purposes. You can pay your mortgage off early, save for retirement, start a college fund, and even have some fun!"

If you saved and invested the $800 every month at 8%, in 15 years you would have over $279,000. If you keep investing it for an additional 20 years, your balance would grow to more than $1.8 million. What a difference being debt free makes! You'll have the opportunity to apply the Accelerator Repayment Plan to your circumstances with the homework assignment this next week.

Additional Tips

Adopt a Proactive Attitude

One of the most significant factors which will influence your success in taking control of your finances is a proactive attitude. Let's take a look at what Sacred Scripture and Church Teaching have to say about attitude. As always, Proverbs is filled with wisdom. Chapter 27:23 says, "Take good care of your flocks, give careful attention to your herds." In chapter 24:30–34, we read, "I passed by the field of the sluggard, by the vineyard of the man without sense; And behold! It was all overgrown with thistles; its surface was covered with nettles, and its stone wall broken down. And as I gazed at it, I reflected; I saw and learned the lesson: A little sleep, a little slumber, a little folding of the arms to rest — then will poverty come upon you like a high-wayman, and want like an armed man."

If you want your finances well organized, a certain level of commitment is required. However, as you see the benefits of reduced frustration and anxiety, I think you'll agree the commitment is worth it.

Build an Orderly File System

Once you've committed to getting organized, the next step is to establish a filing system for all of the paperwork that comes your way (I keep hearing about a paperless society, but I haven't seen it yet!).

I recommend that your files be broken down into two main categories: current and long-term. Since you will refer to your current files frequently, the system works best if they are accessible where you pay bills, such as a file drawer in a desk or a file cabinet close by. On the other hand, you will not need to refer to your long-term files very often so they could be kept in a file cabinet in the garage.

I have found that hanging folders with manila folder inserts work very well for home files. You can find inexpensive plastic crates or portable files that will hold these quite well if you can't afford a filing cabinet.

You can use the following list as a starting point for your own files, but don't be afraid to customize them to fit your own circumstances.

Current Files
- Open Items (bills to pay, unreconciled bank statements).
- Tithing/Almsgiving (church envelopes, correspondence).
- Taxes (current year pay stubs, W-2, and correspondence).
- Education (receipts, correspondence).
- Savings (separate folders for bank accounts, retirement plan, and other investments).
- Housing (separate folders for statements, property taxes, and insurance).
- Automobile (separate folders for each car and insurance).
- Medical Records (separate folders for medical history, current year bills, and your policy).
- Insurance (separate folders for life and disability).
- Debt Payments (separate folders for each credit card or loan).

Long-Term Files
- Employment (employment handbook, résumé).
- Taxes (separate folders for each prior year).
- Savings (separate folders for prior year bank statements, retirement plan, and other investments).
- Housing (separate files for permanent items such as purchase documents, receipts for improvements, and prior-period property taxes).

- Social Security (separate folders for each family member).
- Estate Planning (separate folders for copies of your will or trust and those of other family members as appropriate).

Manage That Checkbook!

When you're at the checkout counter of the grocery store ready to write your check with your baby wiggling in your arms, how often do you just give up on entering the check information in the register, saying you'll get to it when you get home? Then when you get home, all chaos breaks loose and before you know it, you can't remember how much the check was for? For the person who handles the checkbook responsibilities, the frustration level rises as they try to reconstruct what happened.

One of the greatest inventions in the last few years that can go a long way toward eliminating this friction between a husband and wife are carbon-copy checks. When you write the check at the store, an automatic copy remains in your checkbook that can be used to update your register later. I highly recommend them.

It is critical that you reconcile your checkbook each month when your bank statement arrives.

Use the following steps:
- Match all withdrawals and deposits on the bank statement to your check register. Use a check mark in your register to document that the item has been matched. Don't forget to include all ATM and pre-authorized transactions. If any of your documentation doesn't match with the bank's information after double checking, call the bank.
- Document any fees or other charges the bank has made in your checkbook.
- Most bank statements provide a form for reconciling the account on the reverse side of the statement.
- Develop your deposit in transit by listing all deposits that appear in your checkbook which do not appear on your bank statement.
- Develop your outstanding withdrawals by listing all withdrawals that appear in your checkbook which do not appear on the bank statement.
- Bank statement ending balance + deposits in transit − outstanding withdrawals = Checkbook balance. If the total matches your checkbook total, congratulations, you have successfully balanced your checkbook! If it doesn't, retrace your steps asking yourself: Did I make an addition or subtraction error in my checkbook or my list of deposits-in-transit or outstanding withdrawals? Did I miss recording a transaction in the checkbook? (Do a quick review by check number.) Did I properly list outstanding items that carried over from the prior month's reconciliation? If after these steps you still don't reconcile, you may want to call your bank for guidance.

➤ Develop a plan to eliminate your debts with the Accelerator Repayment Plan at www.VeritasFinancialMinistries.com.

➤ Create your filing system.

A THOUGHT FOR THE WEEK

"The borrower is the slave of the lender."

— PROVERBS 22:7

7 STEPS TO BECOMING FINANCIALLY FREE

 STEP ONE   Be a "Steward of Providence"

 STEP TWO   Assess Where You Are – Develop a Plan

 STEP THREE $2,000 Emergency Savings

 STEP FOUR   Eliminate Debt – Accelerate It!

 STEP FIVE   Rainy Day Fund – Six Months' Expenses

 STEP SIX   Review Insurance and Estate Planning Needs

 STEP SEVEN   Save and Invest with a Purpose

HOME SWEET HOME
SMART SPENDING

PRE-SESSION FIVE REQUIREMENTS

➤ Read the following from *7 Steps to Becoming Financially Free*: Chapters 9 and 10.

➤ Complete the following session-five material in the workbook:
   ❏ Review goals for session.
   ❏ Answer discussion topics.
   ❏ Complete reading in practical exercise section.

GOALS — SESSION FIVE

➤ Determine how much house and transportation you can afford and smart ways of financing your home.

➤ Understand the benefits of prepaying your mortgage and the pitfalls of home equity loans.

➤ Understand and apply smart spending principles.

➤ Develop a price list.

➤ Understand insurance basics; complete a Life Insurance Worksheet.

OPENING PRAYER AND INTRODUCTORY VIDEO

Led by group leader.

1. **Read the following references: Luke 14:28-30; Proverbs 24:27.**
Review your cost of housing as a percentage of gross income? How does the percentage compare to the guideline budget? Do you feel that your housing costs allow you to fulfill your other responsibilities?

_____

_____

_____

_____

_____

2. What are the benefits of prepaying the mortgage on your house? How can prepaying your mortgage ease the financial strain of your children's college years and your retirement years? What steps can you take to own your home more quickly?

_____

_____

_____

_____

_____

3. What are the drawbacks to using home equity loans, whether to pay off old credit card debts, making improvements to your house, or other reasons?

_____

_____

_____

_____

_____

4. **Read the following references:** *Catechism* **1809; 1832; 1866; 2342; Genesis 41; Luke 14:28-30.**
Many people think of stewardship only in terms of how much they give. Describe how stewardship involves the use of our remaining resources as well. Why is it important to have a plan for our spending and to spend according to our plan?

_____

_____

_____

_____

_____

5. List at least three things you can do today to start becoming a smart spender.

_____

_____

_____

_____

_____

_____

PRACTICAL EXERCISES

This session's practical exercises are designed to help you set solid goals for your financial future, keeping in mind the 7 Steps to Becoming Financially Free listed at the end of this session. First, we'll review two of the biggest expenses in most budgets – housing and transportation. You'll consider how much you can afford for each of these categories and see how you can save literally tens of thousands of dollars by prepaying your mortgage. We'll also provide a sample price list so you can develop one for your own circumstances. This is a great tool to help you keep your expenses low on key purchases. Then we'll show you how to determine how much life insurance you need, based on the example of the Stewart family.

Determining How Much House and Car You Can Afford

As I mentioned in the book, one of the most important financial decisions you'll make is the purchase of a home. I emphasized the need to keep overall housing costs (including mortgage payment, property taxes, insurance, utilities, gardening, improvements, and all other housing-related costs) within a reasonable percentage of your gross income. Too many people today, especially young families starting out, buy more house than they can afford, making it difficult to meet their other responsibilities such as educating children, saving for the future, and meeting basic medical and insurance needs. The same is true of transportation costs. Auto companies know how to get you into long-term commitments on cars that take too much of your resources. By making good decisions in these two areas, you'll be in a much better position to meet your other responsibilities.

Understanding how much house or car you can afford is a three-step process:

- Determine how much you are spending (or plan to spend if you are a prospective purchaser) on housing/transportation as a percentage of your gross income and compare the results to the guideline budget and in the context of your overall goals. Are you overspending to such a degree that you can't properly meet other responsibilities?

- If you are overspending, consider ways to reduce your housing/transportation costs. Before you make the drastic decision to sell your home or car and downsize, you'll want to first look at how much you are spending on housing/transportation other than your monthly payments. You may be able to generate enough savings in these areas to keep your current house/car.

- If additional savings are necessary, you may need to consider downsizing so that you can lower your monthly payment and your debt level. The loan calculator at www.VeritasFinancialMinistries.com will assist you in considering different scenarios.

Let's go through this exercise with the Stewart family's housing. The table below shows the housing section of the Stewarts' Guideline Budget Review, and the updated budget reflecting the initial adjustments they made. You can see that they started out at 38% of gross income and have lowered it to 34%. That's higher than the goal of 30%, but is a good start.

STEWART FAMILY ANALYSIS OF HOUSING EXPENSES		
	Stewart Family — Initial Budget	Adjusted Budget
Gross Income	**80,000**	**81,500**
Mortgage	18,000	18,000
Insurance	800	800
Taxes	3,000	3,000
Electricity	1,000	800
Gas	900	800
Water	800	700
Gardening	800	200
Housecleaning	0	0
Telephone	1,000	800
Maintenance	1,500	1,000
Pest Control	400	200
Association Dues	0	0
Bottled Water	0	0
Postage	200	100
Miscellaneous	0	0
Improvements	2,000	1,000
Total Costs	30,400	27,400
Cost as % of Gross Income	38%	34%

The Stewarts wanted to see what their monthly payment would have to be in order to bring their overall expenses to the 30% level. 30% of their gross income ($81,500) is $24,450. With adjusted housing costs at $27,400, they need to reduce spending by an additional $2,950. If the only place they can look to achieve this is their mortgage, they need to reduce the annual outlay from $18,000 to about $15,000, or $1,250 per month. The Stewarts wondered what that meant by way of how much house they could afford, so they went to www.VeritasFinancialMinistries.com and used the loan calculator to consider different scenarios. For a standard 30-year fixed loan at 6%, they could afford a loan of $210,000. If they preferred to have a 15-year mortgage, they could afford a loan of about $150,000.

The same type of analysis applies for your transportation costs, except that you would use the transportation section of the Veritas Budget Worksheet to determine how much you are spending as a percentage of your gross income. Use a blank Veritas Budget Worksheet and the tools available at www.VeritasFinancialMinistries.com to complete your own analysis for both housing and transportation.

How to Prepay Your Mortgage

Tom and Patty originally took out a standard fixed 30-year mortgage. Now that they are moving through the *7 Steps to Becoming Financially Free*, they would like to know how they can go about paying the mortgage off more quickly. As you can see above, they just took out a $200,000 mortgage on their home at an interest rate of 6%. Here is how I explained the benefits to prepaying your mortgage in *7 Steps to Becoming Financially Free*:

"The most effective way to build the equity in your home more rapidly is to either take out a 15-year loan or 'prepay' your mortgage. An added benefit to a 15-year loan is that interest rates will normally be about one-half of a percentage point less than similar 30-year loans. Based on the figures presented in the following table, the monthly payment required for the 30-year loan is $1,199.10. But if you took out a 15-year loan, your payment would only increase by $435.07 for a total payment of $1,634.17. You'd end up saving nearly $140,000 in interest!

EXHIBIT 1 — EFFECT OF PREPAYING MORTGAGE		
	30 Year Loan	15 Year Loan
Original Loan Amount	$200,000	$200,000
Interest Rate	6.0%	5.5%
Monthly Payment	$1,199.10	$1,634.17
Difference in Monthly Payments	NA	$435.07
Total Cash Paid During Term of Loan	$431,676.00	$294,150.60
Interest Saved	NA	$137,525.40

"Some financial planners recommend paying your loan off over the standard 30-year period and investing the difference. While this can theoretically make sense, as it does take advantage of compound earnings and the time value of money, it depends on whether you will actually save the difference every month, and whether you can obtain a consistent rate of return at least equal to the interest on your mortgage. My experience tells me that very few people have the discipline to save that discretionary income every month. Instead they end up spending it on regular bills. They really need that tangible goal of owning their house in 15 years along with the forced discipline the 15-year loan gives them in order to stick with the plan. An added benefit of paying your loan off over 15-20 years is that when your children reach college age, the funds that were going to the mortgage will be freed up for educational needs. Financially speaking, you'd be well served to both save consistently and prepay your mortgage.

"While it may seem difficult to come up with the extra money required, a can-do attitude combined with proper planning makes it possible. Most people find that as the years go by, increases in income disappear as a result of increased discretionary spending. Rather than wasting these increases, I recommend a large portion (say 30 percent) be applied as additional payments on your home loan. With the house paid off in 15 years, you'll have the freedom to use the extra funds for other priorities, such as college education for the children or retirement savings.

"Even if you can't afford to increase your payment to a level that would cut the length of your loan in half, I would encourage you to start with some amount—even if only $100 per month. As your income grows, the discipline will be in place to make a wise decision on how the increase should be allocated."

The Stewarts have decided that they would like to pay down their mortgage more quickly than their current 30-year pace. They realize they need to work through some of the other steps to becoming financially free first though. These include setting aside their emergency savings, paying down their consumer debt, and saving their six-month rainy-day fund. Once they have accomplished these, they'll move on to increasing the monthly payment on their mortgage.

Price List

The Price List is a tool that helps you track how much you pay for various items, so that you can be confident that you are getting a good deal. It's important for you to know what a good unit price is, especially on your day-to-day grocery and sundry items. Stores are continually modifying prices, so it's up to you to know which store has the best price on the items you buy at the present time. We rotate through about three stores to do our basic shopping, which allows us to compare unit prices at each of the stores, so we're confident we're doing the best we can to stretch our dollars. The Price List is a key part of helping you do this. In practice, we have found using a small loose-leaf notebook with alphabetical tabs to be the most efficient way to maintain the list. This allows you to quickly look up the items as you move through the store. Make sure you keep a calculator handy each time you go shopping. Visit www.VeritasFinancialMinistries.com to create and maintain your own price list or choose another method that works for you. The key is to know what a good price is based on your past history and this keeps that information at your fingertips. As I mentioned in *7 Steps to Becoming Financially Free*, we first saw this type of analysis in Amy Dacyczyn's *Tightwad Gazette*.

SAMPLE PRICE LIST				
Item Description (Alphabetical)	Store	Container Size	Total Price	Best Price/ Unit of Measure
Applesauce	Store A	106 Oz	$2.99	$.02/Oz
Butter	Store B	4 Pounds	$7.29	$1.82/L
Cinnamon	Store A	18 Oz	$3.75	$.21/Oz
Brand-Name Detergent	Store B	167 Oz	$17.99	$.06/Oz
Organic Peanut Butter	Store C	2 - 26 Oz Jars	$6.99	$.13/Oz

Meeting Your Family's Life Insurance Needs

As I mentioned in *7 Steps to Becoming Financially Free*, term life insurance policies are typically the best way to cover the need for resources in the event of an early death. It's especially important to obtain coverage when you have children, and you should consider having policies in place for both the husband and wife. How much insurance should you purchase? A number of factors go into that determination. You'll want to visit www.VeritasFinancialMinistries.com and use the available worksheet to develop a plan appropriate for your own circumstances. Page 73 shows a sample Life Insurance Worksheet for the Stewart family.

SAMPLE LIFE INSURANCE WORKSHEET

FAMILY RECURRING INCOME REQUIREMENTS (ESTIMATED)	**90,000**
SOURCES OF EXISTING RECURRING INCOME	
Spouse's employment income	—
Investment income	—
Social security	—
Pension or other retirement plan income	—
Other	—
Total recurring income	—
ADDITIONAL INCOME NEEDED	**90,000**
INSURANCE REQUIRED TO MEET RECURRING INCOME NEEDS	**1,125,000**
(Equals additional income needed times 12.5 - assumes 8% return on insurance proceeds)	
NON-RECURRING EXPENSE REQUIREMENTS	
Final expenses	
Final illness	10,000
Burial/funeral	10,000
Estate taxes and settlement expenses	—
Total final expenses	**20,000**
Outstanding debts to be paid off at death	
Credit card/consumer debt	10,000
Auto loans	10,000
Mortgage (2)	200,000
Total outstanding debt	**220,000**
Re-adjustment expenses (to meet needs during transition)	
Child care	—
Additional homemaking help	5,000
Vocational counseling/educational training for surviving spouse	—
Total readjustment expenses	**5,000**
Education expenses (only include here if not part of basic living expenses)	
Estimated tuition charges through college	**200,000**
Total non-recurring expenses	**445,000**
TOTAL INSURANCE REQUIREMENTS BEFORE CONSIDERATION OF AVAILABLE ASSETS	**1,570,000**
ASSETS AVAILABLE TO SUPPORT THE FAMILY	
Proceeds from life insurance already owned	—
Cash and savings	—
Equity in real estate (if survivors will sell)	—
Other investments	—
Retirement plans	12,000
Other sources	—
Total available assets	**12,000**
ADDITIONAL INSURANCE REQUIRED	**1,558,000**

➤ Determine what it would take to pay off your home in half the length of your current mortgage by using the Accelerator Repayment Plan calculator at www.VeritasFinancialMinistries.com.

➤ Create your personal price list.

➤ Visit www.VeritasFinancialMinistries.com and determine the level of life insurance appropriate for your situation.

A THOUGHT FOR THE WEEK

"Temperance is the moral virtue that moderates the attraction of pleasures and provides balance in the use of created goods. It insures the will's mastery over instincts and keeps desires within the limits of what is honorable."

– CATECHISM 1809

7 STEPS TO BECOMING FINANCIALLY FREE

STEP ONE Be a "Steward of Providence"

STEP TWO Assess Where You Are – Develop a Plan

STEP THREE $2,000 Emergency Savings

STEP FOUR Eliminate Debt – Accelerate It!

STEP FIVE Rainy Day Fund – Six Months' Expenses

STEP SIX Review Insurance and Estate Planning Needs

STEP SEVEN Save and Invest with a Purpose

SAVING AND INVESTING WITH A PURPOSE
SIX HABITS FOR SUCCESSFUL INVESTING
PULLING IT ALL TOGETHER

PRE-SESSION SIX REQUIREMENTS

➤ Read the following from *7 Steps to Becoming Financially Free*: Chapters 11 and 12.

➤ Complete the following session-six material in the workbook:
   ❑ Review goals for session.
   ❑ Answer discussion topics.
   ❑ Complete reading in practical exercise section.

GOALS – SESSION SIX

➤ Develop a properly balanced attitude toward saving; avoid an attitude of hoarding.

➤ Learn how to set savings goals, including paying for college and retirement.

➤ Understand investing basics and how to monitor your investment portfolio.

➤ Complete evaluation.

OPENING PRAYER AND INTRODUCTORY VIDEO

Led by group leader.

1. **Read the following reference: Genesis 41.**
Based on this story, what should our attitude be toward saving for the future?

_____

_____

_____

_____

_____

2. **Read the following references: 1 Timothy 6:9-10; Matthew 25:14-30; Proverbs 21:20; Luke 12:16-21.**
These verses describe two extremes toward saving – the failure to save and saving to the point of hoarding – both of which have harmful consequences for our financial and spiritual lives. Which of these extremes do you naturally tend to, and what steps can you take to bring balance to your savings decisions.

_____

_____

_____

_____

_____

3. Explain how compound interest can be your best financial friend or your worst financial foe. Why is it important to begin saving early?

_____

_____

_____

_____

_____

_____

4. What are goals you have (buying a home, paying for college, retirement etc.) that will require saving for the future? Are you setting a lifestyle today that recognizes the need to save for those future goals? If not, what steps will you take to begin saving for those goals?

_____

_____

_____

_____

_____

_____

5. **Read the following references: Proverbs 13:11; 21:5; 28:20; 28:22; *Catechism* 2413.**
Describe how these verses discourage involvement with "get-rich-quick" schemes, including questionable business ventures and destructive gambling.

_____

_____

_____

_____

_____

6. **Read Proverbs 27:23.**
Why is it important for people to understand what they are investing in? Why are mutual funds a good investment path for many people today? Why is it important for you to periodically monitor the performance of your investments? What are some of the key measures that you will want to track over time?

_____

_____

_____

_____

_____

*I*n this final session, using the Stewart family as an example, we'll look at two common future needs — determining how much they'll need to pay for their kids' college education and how much they'll need to save for retirement. We'll also review the Stewarts' Investment Portfolio Tracker to see how they monitor their investments and be sure they are on track to meet their goals. By using the calculators at www.VeritasFinancialMinistries.com, you'll be able to consider each of these needs as they relate to your own scenario and develop amounts you should be including in your budget for these purposes.

Paying for College

As I noted in *7 Steps to Becoming Financially Free*, for many of our children, a Catholic higher education is an integral part of their development into young adults who are mature in their love of God and are ready to apply their talents in the world today. It seems as though the need for such an education increases each year, and unfortunately the costs continue to increase as well. One of the keys to funding your children's college years without having them leave school

SAMPLE COLLEGE PLANNING WORKSHEET	
Estimated Annual College Expenses (current dollars)	25,000
# Children Attending (current ages 14; 10; 6 and 2)	4
Total Estimated College Expenses (current dollars)	400,000
Total Estimated College Expenses (inflation adjusted at 4%)	638,000
Less: Anticipated Resources During College Years	
Current allocation from budget (18,000 per year times 16 college years) (Note 1)	288,000
Work study (3,000 for each college year times 16 college years — inflation adjusted)	71,000
Summer earnings (2,000 per college year times 16 college years — inflation adjusted)	47,000
Scholarships and Grants	—
College Loans (15,000 per student in current dollars — inflation adjusted)	86,717
TOTAL	492,717
Funding Gap	145,283
Number of Years to Save (including college years)	20
Monthly Savings Required	500
Annual Savings Required (monthly savings required times 12)	6,000
Annual Gross Income	81,500
Annual Savings as % of Annual Gross Income	7.4%

Note: This is the amount parents expect to contribute toward college expenses from their budget during the college years. By having the mortgage paid off, it is easier to make a more substantial allocation toward college education.

weighed down with too much debt is to develop a plan early. One aspect of that plan may be the pre-paying of your mortgage so that when your oldest child reaches the college years, the mortgage payment can be reallocated to college expenses. At the same time, it makes sense to take advantage of the time value of money and set aside savings for future education needs. By starting when your little one is in the womb, you'll increase your child's options down the road.

Don't get discouraged over the cost of educating your children. For those with modest incomes, remember that you are only called to do the best you can with the resources you have. Encourage your children to study hard so they will qualify for scholarships. Most schools take need into account as part of the funding process. Visit www.VeritasFinancialMinistries.com to consider different alternatives for your own situation.

The Stewart family has four children and has set a goal that will allow each child to attend a four year Catholic university, and finish school with no more than $15,000 in student loans. There are many approaches that can be taken to handle the funding for such a goal, but the worksheet on page 79 shows one approach the Stewart family can use to take some of the sting out of paying for college.

Planning for Retirement

When you consistently apply the 7 Steps to Becoming Financially Free, you develop a financial foundation that frees you up to be of service in God's work, especially during your retirement years. While each situation warrants reviewing the particular circumstances, a common rule of thumb is that you'll need 80 percent of your pre-retirement income during your retirement years. Just as with funding college, there are many approaches that can be taken by way of retirement savings plans, but the key is to actually save consistently during your working

SAMPLE RETIREMENT PLANNING WORKSHEET	
Current Age	38
Estimated Retirement Age	70
Current Gross Income	81,500
Inflation Adjusted Income at Retirement	204,000
Estimated Retirement Income Need as % of Current Income	80%
Estimated Retirement Income — Dollars	163,200
Estimated Investment Return	10%
Investment Necessary at Retirement (assumes keeping principal intact)	1,632,000
Current Retirement Savings	12,000
Funding Gap	1,620,000
Monthly Savings Required to Meet Investment Goal	520
Annual Savings Required to Meet Investment Goal	6,240
Annual Savings as % of Current Annual Gross Income	8%

years, so that you'll have adequate funds to meet your retirement needs. While your own retirement goals will vary, the Stewart family has set a goal of saving enough so that they can use the investment income to live on, while not depleting the base investment principal. They would like to see that amount passed on to the children as an inheritance, after giving a tenth to their favorite charities. On page 80 is an example of what the Stewarts' retirement planning might look like. Visit www.VeritasFinancialMinistries.com to consider your own situation.

Savings and Investment Monitor

Having gone through the exercise of determining savings needs for college and retirement, the Stewarts now need to not only save and invest the money consistently, but they need to monitor the results of those investments to make sure they are on track to grow sufficiently (remember they need to average an 8% annual return on the invested funds) to meet the corresponding need. As mentioned in *7 Steps to Becoming Financially Free*, there is an array of free resources available via the internet to help you monitor your investments. One very helpful site is www.morningstar.com. The Stewarts have found that the following schedule provides them the information they need. They update it every three months at the end of each calendar quarter.

SAMPLE INVESTMENT PORTFOLIO TRACKER									
Account and Fund Name	Investment Advisor	Ticker Symbol	YTD Market Value $	Rate of Return %	Exp Ratio %	Net Return	3 Yr Return %	5 Yr Return %	10 Yr Return %
Retirement Plan Account									
Lg-Cap Blend Sep Acct	Advisor A	AAAAA	3,000	6.2%	0.77%	5.4%	10.9%	NA	NA
SmCap Value Sep Acct	Advisor A	BBBBB	2,000	10.1%	1.02%	9.1%	20.0%	NA	NA
SmCap Stk Idx Sep Acct	Advisor B	CCCCC	2,000	10.2%	0.40%	9.8%	20.8%	13.0%	NA
LgCap Growth I Sep Acct	Advisor B	DDDDD	3,000	9.5%	0.73%	8.7%	10.5%	NA	NA
SmCap Growth II Sep Acct	Advisor B	EEEEE	2,000	9.0%	1.01%	8.0%	17.4%	NA	NA
Total Retirement Account			**12,000**	**8.8%**	**0.8%**	**8.0%**			

➤ Visit www.VeritasFinancialMinistries.com and determine how much you should be saving for your retirement and for the college education of your children.

➤ Develop your own investment-monitoring report using the guide in the workbook.

➤ Complete the evaluation form at the back of the workbook or online at www.VeritasFinancialMinistries.com. This helps us make adjustments to the materials that will benefit those going through them in the future.

A PARTING THOUGHT

"To begin is for everyone, to persevere is for saints."

– St. Josemaría Escrivá

7 STEPS TO BECOMING FINANCIALLY FREE

STEP ONE   Be a "Steward of Providence"

STEP TWO   Assess Where You Are – Develop a Plan

STEP THREE $2,000 Emergency Savings

STEP FOUR   Eliminate Debt – Accelerate It!

STEP FIVE   Rainy Day Fund – Six Months' Expenses

STEP SIX   Review Insurance and Estate Planning Needs

STEP SEVEN   Save and Invest with a Purpose

BIBLE AND *CATECHISM* REFERENCES

Discussion Topic 1

Isaiah 55:8-9 — For my thoughts are not your thoughts, neither are your ways my ways, says the LORD. For as the heavens are higher than the earth, so are my ways higher than your ways and my thoughts than your thoughts.

Discussion Topic 2

Deuteronomy 10:14 — Behold, to the LORD your God belong heaven and the heaven of heavens, the earth with all that is in it.

1 Chronicles 29:11-12 — Thine, O LORD, is the greatness, and the power, and the glory, and the victory, and the majesty; for all that is in the heavens and in the earth is thine; thine is the kingdom, O LORD, and thou art exalted as head above all. Both riches and honor come from thee, and thou rulest over all. In thy hand are power and might; and in thy hand it is to make great and to give strength to all.

Psalm 24:1 — The earth is the LORD's and the fullness thereof, the world and those who dwell therein.

1 Corinthians 4:1-2 — This is how one should regard us, as servants of Christ and stewards of the mysteries of God. Moreover it is required of stewards that they be found trustworthy.

Catechism 2404 — "In his use of things man should regard the external goods he legitimately owns not merely exclusive to himself but common to others also, in the sense that they can benefit others as well as himself" (GS 69 § 1). The ownership of any property makes its holder a steward of Providence, with the task of making it fruitful and communicating its benefits to others, first of all his family.

Luke 14:33 — So therefore, whoever of you does not renounce all that he has cannot be my disciple.

Discussion Topic 3

John 3:16 — For God so loved the world that he gave his only Son, that whoever believes in him should not perish but have eternal life.

Mark 8:36 — For what does it profit a man, to gain the whole world and forfeit his life?

Matthew 6:24 — No one can serve two masters; for either he will hate the one and love the other, or he will be devoted to the one and despise the other. You cannot serve God and mammon.

Job 1:21 — "Naked I came from my mother's womb, and naked shall I return; the LORD gave, and the LORD has taken away; blessed be the name of the LORD."

Discussion Topic 4

Matthew 5: 1-12 — Seeing the crowds, he went up on the mountain, and when he sat down his disciples came to him. And he opened his mouth and taught them, saying: "Blessed are the poor in spirit, for theirs is the kingdom of heaven. "Blessed are those who mourn, for they shall be comforted. "Blessed are the meek, for they shall inherit the earth. "Blessed are those who hunger and thirst for righteousness, for they shall be satisfied. "Blessed are the merciful, for they shall obtain mercy. "Blessed are the pure in heart, for they shall see God. "Blessed are the peacemakers, for they shall be called sons of God. "Blessed are those who are persecuted for righteousness' sake, for theirs is the kingdom of heaven. "Blessed are you when men revile you and persecute you and utter all kinds of evil against you falsely on my account. Rejoice and be glad, for your reward is great in heaven, for so men persecuted the prophets who were before you."

Matthew 5:48 — "You, therefore, must be perfect, as your heavenly Father is perfect."

Catechism 2015 — The way of perfection passes by way of the Cross.

Catechism 459 — The Word became flesh *to be our model of holiness.*

Matthew 7:24-27 — "Every one then who hears these words of mine and does them will be like a wise man who built his house upon the rock; and the rain fell, and the floods came, and the winds blew and beat upon that house, but it did not fall, because it had been founded on the rock. And every one who hears these words of mine and does not do them will be like a foolish man who built his house upon the sand; and the rain fell, and the floods came, and the winds blew and beat against that house, and it fell; and great was the fall of it."

John 2:5 — "Do whatever he tells you."

John 8:12 — Again Jesus spoke to them, saying, "I am the light of the world; he who follows me will not walk in darkness, but will have the light of life."

John 12:26 — "If anyone serves me, he must follow me; and where I am, there shall my servant be also; if any one serves me, the Father will honor him."

Discussion Topic 6

Ephesians 6:10-18 — Finally, be strong in the Lord and in the strength of his might. Put on the whole armor of God, that you may be able to stand against the wiles of the devil. For we are not contending against flesh and blood, but against the principalities, against the powers, against the world rulers of this present darkness, against the spiritual hosts of wickedness in the heavenly places. Therefore take the whole armor of God, that you may be able to withstand in the evil day, and having done all, to stand. Stand therefore, having girded your loins with truth, and having put on the breastplate of righteousness, and having shod your feet with the equipment of the gospel of peace; above all taking the shield of faith, with which you can quench all the flaming darts of the evil one. And take the helmet of salvation, and the sword of the Spirit, which is the word of God. Pray at all times in the Spirit, with all prayer and supplication. To that end keep alert with all perseverance, making supplication for all the saints.

1 Timothy 4:7-8 — Train yourself in godliness; for while bodily training is of some value, godliness is of value in every way, as it holds promise for the present life and also for the life to come.

Catechism 1866 — Vices can be classified according to the virtues they oppose, or also be linked to the *capital sins* which Christian experience has distinguished, following St. John Cassian and St. Gregory the Great. They are called "capital" because they engender other sins, other vices. (Cf. St. Gregory the Great, *Moralia in Job*, 31, 45: PL 76, 621A.) They are pride, avarice, envy, wrath, lust, gluttony, and sloth or acedia.

BIBLE AND *CATECHISM* REFERENCES — SESSION TWO

Discussion Topic 1

Catechism 1601 — "The matrimonial covenant, by which a man and a woman establish between themselves a partnership of the whole of life, is by its nature ordered toward the good of the spouses and the procreation and education of offspring; this covenant between baptized persons has been raised by Christ to the dignity of a sacrament" (CIC, can. 1055 § 1; cf. GS 48 § 1).

Catechism 1641 — Grace proper to the sacrament of Matrimony is intended to perfect the couple's love and to strengthen their indissoluble unity. By this grace they "help one another to attain holiness in their married life and in welcoming and educating their children" (LG 11 § 2; cf. LG 41).

Catechism 1666 — The family home is rightly called "the domestic church," a community of grace and prayer, a school of human virtues and of Christian charity.

Discussion Topic 2

1 Corinthians 13:1-13 — If I speak in the tongues of men and of angels, but have not love, I am a noisy gong or a clanging cymbal. And if I have prophetic powers, and understand all mysteries and all knowledge, and if I have all faith, so as to remove mountains, but have not love, I am nothing. If I give away all I have, and if I deliver my body to be burned, but have not love, I gain nothing. Love is patient and kind; love is not jealous or boastful; it is not arrogant or rude. Love does not insist on its own way; it is not irritable or resentful; it does not rejoice at wrong, but rejoices in the right. Love bears all things, believes all things, hopes all things, endures all things. Love never ends; as for prophecies, they will pass away; as for tongues, they will cease; as for knowledge, it will pass away. For our knowledge is imperfect and our prophecy is imperfect; but when the perfect comes, the imperfect will pass away. When I was a child, I spoke like a child, I thought like a child, I reasoned like a child; when I became a man, I gave up childish ways. For now we see in a mirror dimly, but then face to face. Now I know in part; then I shall understand fully, even as I have been fully understood. So faith, hope, love abide, these three; but the greatest of these is love.

Ephesians 5:21-33 — Be subject to one another out of reverence for Christ. Wives, be subject to your husbands, as to the Lord. For the husband is the head of the wife as Christ is the head of the church, his body, and is himself its Savior. As the church is subject to Christ, so let wives also be subject in everything to their husbands. Husbands, love your wives, as Christ loved the church and gave himself up for her, that he might sanctify her, having cleansed her by the washing of water with the word, that he might present the church to himself in splendor, without spot or wrinkle or any such thing, that she might be holy and without blemish. Even so husbands should love their wives as their own bodies. He who loves his wife loves himself. For no man ever hates his own flesh, but nourishes and cherishes it, as Christ does the church, because we are members of his body. "For this reason a man shall leave his father and mother and be joined to his wife, and the two shall become one flesh." This mystery is a profound one, and I am saying that it refers to Christ and the church; however, let each one of you love his wife as himself, and let the wife see that she respects her husband.

Genesis 2:24 — Therefore a man leaves his father and his mother and cleaves to his wife, and they become one flesh.

Mark 10:9 — What therefore God has joined together, let not man put asunder.

Discussion Topic 3

1 Corinthians 12:4-7 — Now there are varieties of gifts, but the same Spirit; and there are varieties of service, but the same Lord; and there are varieties of working, but it is the same God who inspires them all in everyone. To each is given the manifestation of the Spirit for the common good.

Discussion Topic 4

Psalm 32:8 — I will instruct you and teach you the way you should go; I will counsel you with my eye upon you.

Psalm 119:105 — Thy word is a lamp to my feet and a light to my path.

Proverbs 12:15 — The way of a fool is right in his own eyes, but a wise man listens to advice.

Proverbs 13:10 — By insolence the heedless make strife, but with those who take advice is wisdom.

Proverbs 15:22 — Without counsel plans go wrong, but with many advisers they succeed.

Discussion Topic 5

Christifideles Laici 59 — There cannot be two parallel lives in their existence: on the one hand, the so-called "spiritual" life, with its values and demands; and on the other, the so-called "secular" life, that is life in a family, at work, in social relationships, in the responsibilities of public life and in culture.

Catechism 2427 — *Human work* proceeds directly from persons created in the image of God and called to prolong the work of creation by subduing the earth, both with and for one another. (Cf. Gen 1:28; GS 34; CA 31.) Hence work is a duty: "If any one will not work, let him not eat" (2 Thess 3:10; cf. 1 Thess 4:11). Work honors the Creator's gifts and the talents received from him. It can also be redemptive.

Psalm 127:1-2 — Unless the LORD builds the house, those who build it labor in vain. Unless the LORD watches over the city, the watchman stays awake in vain. It is in vain that you rise up early and go late to rest, eating the bread of anxious toil, for he gives to his beloved sleep.

Philippians 2:3-8 — Do nothing from selfishness or conceit, but in humility count others better than yourselves. Let each of you look not only to his own interests, but also to the interests of others. Have this mind among yourselves, which was in Christ Jesus, who, though he was in the form of God, did not count equality with God a thing to be grasped, but emptied himself, taking the form of a servant, being born in the likeness of men. And being found in human form he humbled himself, and became obedient unto death, even death on a cross.

Discussion Topic 6

Exodus 18:13-27 — On the morrow Moses sat to judge the people, and the people stood about Moses from morning till evening. When Moses' father-in-law saw all that he was doing for the people, he said, "What is this that you are doing for the people? Why do you sit alone, and all the people stand about you from morning till evening?" And Moses said to his father-in-law, "Because the people come to me to inquire of God; when they have a dispute, they come to me and I decide between a man and his neighbor, and I make them know the statutes of God and his decisions." Moses' father-in-law said to him, "What you are doing is not good. You and the people with you will wear yourselves out, for the thing is too heavy for you; you are not able to perform it alone. Listen now to my voice; I will give you counsel, and God be with you! You shall represent the people before God, and bring their cases to God; and you shall teach them the statutes and the decisions, and make them know the way in which they must walk and what they must do. Moreover choose able men from all the people, such as fear God, men who are trustworthy and who hate a bribe; and place such men over the people as rulers of thousands, of hundreds, of fifties, and of tens. And let them judge the people at all times; every great matter they shall bring to you, but any small matter they shall decide themselves; so it will be easier for you, and they will bear the burden with you. If you do this, and God so commands you, then you will be able to endure, and all this people also will go to their place in peace." So Moses gave heed to the voice of his father-in-law and did all that he had said. Moses chose able men out of all Israel, and made them heads over the people, rulers of thousands, of hundreds, of fifties, and of tens. And they judged the people at all times; hard cases they brought to Moses, but any small matter they decided themselves. Then Moses let his father-in-law depart, and he went his way to his own country.

Exodus 20: 9-11 — Six days you shall labor, and do all your work; but the seventh day is a sabbath to the LORD your God; in it you shall not do any work, you, or your son, or your daughter, your manservant, or your maidservant, or your cattle, or the sojourner who is within your gates; for in six days the LORD made heaven and earth, the sea, and all that is in them, and rested the seventh day; therefore the LORD blessed the sabbath day and hallowed it.

Catechism **2184-2187** — Just as God "rested on the seventh day from all his work which he had done," (Gen 2:2) human life has a rhythm of work and rest. The institution of the Lord's Day helps everyone enjoy adequate rest and leisure to cultivate their familial, cultural, social, and religious lives. (Cf. GS 67 § 3.) On Sundays and other holy days of obligation, the faithful are to refrain from engaging in work or activities that hinder the worship owed to God, the joy proper to the Lord's Day, the performance of the works of mercy, and the appropriate relaxation of mind and body. (Cf. CIC, can. 1247.) Family needs or important social service can legitimately excuse from the obligation of Sunday rest. The faithful should see to it that legitimate excuses do not lead to habits prejudicial to religion, family life, and health. "The charity of truth seeks holy leisure; the necessity of charity accepts just work" (St. Augustine, *De civ. Dei* 19, 19: PL 41, 647). Those Christians who have leisure should be mindful of their brethren who have the same needs and the same rights, yet cannot rest from work because of poverty and misery. Sunday is traditionally consecrated by Christian piety to good works and humble service of the sick, the infirm, and the elderly. Christians will also sanctify Sunday by devoting time and care to their families and relatives, often difficult to do on other days of the week. Sunday is a time for reflection, silence, cultivation of the mind, and meditation which furthers the growth of the Christian interior life. Sanctifying Sundays and holy days requires a common effort. Every Christian should avoid making unnecessary demands on others that would hinder them from observing the Lord's Day. Traditional activities (sport, restaurants, etc.), and social necessities (public services, etc.), require some people to work on Sundays, but everyone should still take care to set aside sufficient time for leisure. With temperance and charity the faithful will see to it that they avoid the excesses and violence sometimes associated with popular leisure activities. In spite of economic constraints, public authorities should ensure citizens a time intended for rest and divine worship. Employers have a similar obligation toward their employees.

BIBLE AND *CATECHISM* REFERENCES — SESSION THREE

Discussion Topic 1

Catechism 2221 — The fecundity of conjugal love cannot be reduced solely to the procreation of children, but must extend to their moral education and their spiritual formation. "The *role of parents in education* is of such importance that it is almost impossible to provide an adequate substitute" (GE 3). The right and the duty of parents to educate their children are primordial and inalienable. (Cf. FC 36.)

Deuteronomy 6:6-7 — "And these words which I command you this day shall be upon your heart; and you shall teach them diligently to your children, and shall talk of them when you sit in your house, and when you walk by the way, and when you lie down, and when you rise."

Proverbs 22:6 — Train up a child in the way he should go, and when he is old he will not depart from it.

Discussion Topic 2

Malachi 3:7-10 — "From the days of your fathers you have turned aside from my statutes and have not kept them. Return to me, and I will return to you, says the LORD of hosts. But you say, 'How shall we return?' Will man rob God? Yet you are robbing me. But you say, 'How are we robbing thee?' In your tithes and offerings. You are cursed with a curse, for you are robbing me; the whole nation of you. Bring the full tithes into the storehouse, that there may be food in my house; and thereby put me to the test, says the LORD of hosts, if I will not open the windows of heaven for you and pour down for you an overflowing blessing."

Matthew 25:35-40 — "'For I was hungry and you gave me food, I was thirsty and you gave me drink, I was a stranger and you welcomed me, I was naked and you clothed me, I was sick and you visited me, I was in prison and you came to me.' Then the righteous will answer him, 'Lord, when did we see thee hungry and feed thee, or thirsty and give thee drink? And when did we see thee a stranger and welcome thee, or naked and clothe thee? And when did we see thee sick or in prison and visit thee?' And the King will answer them, 'Truly, I say to you, as you did it to one of the least of these my brethren, you did it to me.'"

1 Corinthians 13:3 — If I give away all I have, and if I deliver my body to be burned, but have not love, I gain nothing.

Discussion Topic 3

Leviticus 27:30 — "All the tithe of the land, whether of the seed of the land or of the fruit of the trees, is the LORD's; it is holy to the LORD."

Proverbs 3:9 — Honor the LORD with your substance and with the first fruits of all your produce.

Matthew 23:23 — "Woe to you, scribes and Pharisees, hypocrites! for you tithe mint and dill and cummin, and have neglected the weightier matters of the law, justice and mercy and faith; these you ought to have done, without neglecting the others."

2 Corinthians 9:6-7 — The point is this: he who sows sparingly will also reap sparingly, and he who sows bountifully will also reap bountifully. Each one must do as he has made up his mind, not reluctantly or under compulsion, for God loves a cheerful giver.

St. Irenaeus (Office of Readings – 2nd Saturday in Ordinary Time) — Thus the people of Israel used to dedicate tithes of their possessions. But those who have been given freedom devote what they possess to the Lord's use. They give it all to him, not simply what is of lesser value, cheerfully and freely because they hope for greater things, like the widow who put into God's treasury her whole livelihood.

Code of Canon Law 222 — The Christian faithful are obliged to assist with the needs of the Church so that the Church has what is necessary for divine worship, for the works of the apostolate and of charity, and for the decent support of ministers. They are also obliged . . . to assist the poor from their own resources.

Discussion Topic 4

1 Kings 17:7-16 — And after a while the brook dried up, because there was no rain in the land. Then the word of the LORD came to him, "Arise, go to Zarephath, which belongs to Sidon, and dwell there. Behold, I have commanded a widow there to feed you." So he arose and went to Zarephath; and when he came to the gate of the city, behold, a widow was there gathering sticks; and he called to her and said, "Bring me a little water in a vessel, that I may drink." And as she was going to bring it, he called to her and said, "Bring me a morsel of bread in your hand." And she said, "As the LORD your God lives, I have nothing baked, only a handful of meal in a jar, and a little oil in a cruse; and now, I am gathering a couple of sticks, that I may go in and prepare it for myself and my son, that we may eat it, and die." And Elijah said to her, "Fear not; go and do as you have said; but first make me a little cake of it and bring it to me, and afterward make for yourself and your son. For thus says the LORD the God of Israel, 'The jar of meal shall not be spent, and the cruse of oil shall not fail, until the day that the LORD sends rain upon the earth.'" And she went and did as Elijah said; and she, and he, and her household ate for many days. The jar of meal was not spent, neither did the cruse of oil fail, according to the word of the LORD which he spoke by Elijah.

2 Kings 4:1-7 — Now the wife of one of the sons of the prophets cried to Elisha, "Your servant my husband is dead; and you know that your servant feared the LORD, but the creditor has come to take my two children to be his slaves." And Elisha said to her, "What shall I do for you? Tell me; what have you in the house?" And she said, "Your maidservant has nothing in the house, except a jar of oil." Then he said, "Go outside, borrow vessels of all your neighbors, empty vessels and not too few. Then go in, and shut the door upon yourself and your sons, and pour into all these vessels; and when one is full, set it aside." So she went from him and shut the door upon herself and her sons; and as she poured they brought the vessels to her. When the vessels were full, she said to her son, "Bring me another vessel." And he said to her, "There is not another." Then the oil stopped flowing. She came and told the man of God, and he said, "Go, sell the oil and pay your debts, and you and your sons can live on the rest."

Matthew 14:13-21 — Now when Jesus heard this, he withdrew from there in a boat to a lonely place apart. But when the crowds heard it, they followed him on foot from the towns. As he went ashore he saw a great throng; and he had compassion on them, and healed their sick. When it was evening, the disciples came to him and said, "This is a lonely place, and the day is now over; send the crowds away to go into the villages and buy food for themselves." Jesus said, "They need not go away; you give them something to eat." They said to him, "We have only five loaves here and two fish." And he said, "Bring them here to me." Then he ordered the crowds to sit down on the grass; and taking the five loaves and the two fish he looked up to heaven, and blessed, and broke and gave the loaves to the disciples, and the disciples gave them to the crowds. And they all ate and were satisfied. And they took up twelve baskets full of the broken pieces left over. And those who ate were about five thousand men, besides women and children.

BIBLE AND *CATECHISM* REFERENCES — SESSION FOUR

Discussion Topic 2

Luke 14:28-30 — "For which of you, desiring to build a tower, does not first sit down and count the cost, whether he has enough to complete it? Otherwise, when he has laid a foundation, and is not able to finish, all who see it begin to mock him, saying, 'This man began to build, and was not able to finish.'"

Discussion Topic 4

Deuteronomy 15:5-6 — "If only you will obey the voice of the LORD your God, being careful to do all this commandment which I command you this day. For the LORD your God will bless you, as he promised you, and you shall lend to many nations, but you shall not borrow; and you shall rule over many nations, but they shall not rule over you."

Proverbs 22:7 — The rich rules over the poor, and the borrower is the slave of the lender.

Proverbs 22:26-27 — Be not one of those who give pledges, who become surety for debts. If you have nothing with which to pay, why should your bed be taken from under you?

Proverbs 6:1-5 — My son, if you have become surety for your neighbor, have given your pledge for a stranger; if you are snared in the utterance of your lips, caught in the words of your mouth; then do this, my son, and save yourself, for you have come into your neighbor's power: go, hasten, and importune your neighbor. Give your eyes no sleep and your eyelids no slumber; save yourself like a gazelle from the hunter, like a bird from the hand of the fowler.

Habakkuk 2:6-7 — Shall not all these take up their taunt against him, in scoffing derision of him, and say, "Woe to him who heaps up what is not his own – for how long? – and loads himself with pledges!" Will not your debtors suddenly arise, and those awake who will make you tremble? Then you will be booty for them.

Catechism 2410-2411 — *Promises* must be kept and *contracts* strictly observed to the extent that the commitments made in them are morally just.... Contracts are subject to *commutative justice* which regulates exchanges between persons and between institutions in accordance with a strict respect for their rights. Commutative justice obliges strictly; it requires safeguarding property rights, paying debts, and fulfilling obligations freely contracted.

Discussion Topic 7

1 Timothy 5:8 — If any one does not provide for his relatives, and especially for his own family, he has disowned the faith and is worse than an unbeliever.

Proverbs 13:22 — A good man leaves an inheritance to his children's children.

Proverbs 20:21 — An inheritance gotten hastily in the beginning will in the end not be blessed.

BIBLE AND *CATECHISM* REFERENCES — SESSION FIVE

Discussion Topic 1

Luke 14:28-29 — "For which of you, desiring to build a tower, does not first sit down and count the cost, whether he has enough to complete it? Otherwise, when he has laid a foundation, and is not able to finish, all who see it begin to mock him, saying, 'This man began to build, and was not able to finish.'"

Proverbs 24:27 — Prepare your work outside, get everything ready for you in the field; and after that build your house.

Discussion Topic 4

Catechism 1809 — *Temperance* is the moral virtue that moderates the attraction of pleasures and provides balance in the use of created goods. It ensures the will's mastery over instincts and keeps desires within the limits of what is honorable.

Catechism 1832 — The *fruits* of the Spirit are perfections that the Holy Spirit forms in us as the fruits of eternal glory. The tradition of the Church lists twelve of them: "charity, joy, peace, patience, kindness, goodness, generosity, gentleness, faithfulness, modesty, self-control, chastity" (Gal 5:22-23 [Vulg.]).

Catechism 1866 — Vices can be classified according to the virtues they oppose, or also be linked to the *capital sins* which Christian experience has distinguished, following St. John Cassian and St. Gregory the Great. They are called "capital" because they engender other sins, other vices. (Cf. St. Gregory the Great, *Moralia in Job*, 31, 45: PL 76, 621A.) They are pride, avarice, envy, wrath, lust, gluttony, and sloth or acedia.

Catechism 2342 — Self-mastery is a *long and exacting work*. One can never consider it acquired once and for all. It presupposes renewed effort at all stages of life. (Cf. Titus 2:1-6.)

Genesis 41 — After two whole years, Pharaoh dreamed that he was standing by the Nile, and behold, there came up out of the Nile seven cows sleek and fat, and they fed in the reed grass. And behold, seven other cows, gaunt and thin, came up out of the Nile after them, and stood by the other cows on the bank of the Nile. And the gaunt and thin cows ate up the seven sleek and fat cows. And Pharaoh awoke. And he fell asleep and dreamed a second time; and behold, seven ears of grain, plump and good, were growing on one stalk. And behold, after them sprouted seven ears, thin and blighted by the east wind. And the thin ears swallowed up the seven plump and full ears. And Pharaoh awoke, and behold, it was a dream. So in the morning his spirit was troubled; and he sent and called for all the magicians of Egypt and all its wise men; and Pharaoh told them his dream, but there was none who could interpret it to Pharaoh. Then the chief butler said to Pharaoh, "I remember my faults today. When Pharaoh was angry with his servants, and put me and the chief baker in custody in the house of the captain of the guard, we dreamed on the same night, he and I, each having a dream with its own meaning. A young Hebrew was there with us, a servant of the captain of the guard; and when we told him, he interpreted our dreams to us, giving an interpretation to each man according to his dream. And as he interpreted to us, so it came to pass; I was restored to my office, and the baker was hanged." Then Pharaoh sent and called Joseph, and they brought him hastily out of the dungeon; and when he had shaved himself and changed his clothes, he came in before Pharaoh. And Pharaoh said to Joseph, "I have had a dream, and there is no one who can interpret it; and I have heard it said of you that when you hear a dream you can interpret it." Joseph answered Pharaoh, "It is not in me; God will give Pharaoh a favorable answer." Then Pharaoh said to Joseph, "Behold, in my dream I was standing on the banks of the Nile; and seven cows, fat and sleek, came up out of the Nile and fed in the reed grass; and seven other cows came up after them, poor and very gaunt and thin, such as I had never seen in all the land of Egypt. And the thin and gaunt cows ate up the first seven fat cows, but when they had eaten them no one would have known that they had eaten them, for they were still as gaunt as at the beginning. Then I awoke. I also saw in my dream seven ears growing on one stalk, full and good; and seven ears, withered, thin, and blighted by the east wind, sprouted after them, and the thin ears swallowed up the seven good ears. And I told it to the magicians, but there was no one who could explain it to me." Then Joseph said to Pharaoh, "The dream of Pharaoh is one; God has revealed to Pharaoh what he is about to do. The seven good cows are seven years, and the seven good ears are seven years; the dream is one. The seven lean and gaunt cows that came up after them are seven years, and the seven empty ears blighted by the east wind are also seven years of famine. It is as I told Pharaoh, God has shown to Pharaoh what he is about to do. There will come seven years of great plenty throughout all the land of Egypt, but after them there will arise seven years of famine, and all the plenty will be forgotten in the land of Egypt; the famine will consume the land, and the plenty will be unknown in the land by reason of that famine which will follow, for it will be very grievous. And the doubling of Pharaoh's dream means that the thing is fixed by God, and God will shortly bring it to pass. Now therefore let Pharaoh select a man discreet and wise, and set him over the land of Egypt. Let Pharaoh proceed to appoint overseers over the land, and take the fifth part of the produce of the land of Egypt during the seven plenteous years. And let them gather all the food of these good years that are coming, and lay up grain under the authority of Pharaoh for food in the cities, and let them keep it. That food shall be a reserve for the land against the seven years of famine which are to befall the land of Egypt, so that the land may not perish through the famine." This proposal seemed good to Pharaoh and to all his servants. And Pharaoh said to his servants, "Can we find such a man as this, in whom is the Spirit of God?" So Pharaoh said to Joseph, "Since God has shown you all this, there is none so discreet and wise as you are; you shall be over my house, and all my people shall order themselves as you command; only as regards the throne will I be greater than you." And Pharaoh said to Joseph, "Behold, I have set you over all the land of Egypt." Then Pharaoh took his signet ring from his hand and put it on Joseph's hand, and arrayed him in garments of fine linen, and put a gold chain about his neck; and he made him to ride in his second chariot; and they cried before him, "Bow the knee!" Thus he set him over all the land of Egypt. Moreover Pharaoh said to Joseph, "I am Pharaoh, and without your consent no man shall lift up hand or foot in all the land of Egypt." And Pharaoh called Joseph's name Zaphenath-paneah; and he gave him in marriage Asenath, the daughter of Potiphera priest of On. So Joseph went out over the land of Egypt. Joseph was thirty years old when he entered the service of Pharaoh king of Egypt. And Joseph went out from the presence of Pharaoh, and went through all the land of Egypt. During the seven plenteous years the earth brought forth abundantly, and he gathered up all the food of the seven years when there was plenty in the land of Egypt, and stored up food in the cities; he stored up in every city the food from the fields around it. And Joseph stored up grain in great abundance, like the sand of the sea, until he ceased to measure it, for it could not be measured. Before the year of famine came, Joseph had two sons, whom Asenath, the daughter of Potiphera priest of On, bore to him. Joseph called the name of the first-born Manasseh, "For," he said, "God has made me forget all my hardship and all my father's house." The name of the second he called Ephraim, "For God has made me fruitful in the land of my affliction." The seven years of plenty that prevailed in the land of Egypt came to an end; and the seven years of famine began to come, as Joseph had said. There was famine in all lands; but in all the land of Egypt there was bread. When all the land of Egypt was famished, the people cried to Pharaoh for bread; and Pharaoh said to all the Egyptians, "Go to Joseph; what he says to you, do." So when the famine had spread over all the land, Joseph opened all the storehouses, and sold to the Egyptians, for the famine was severe in the land of Egypt. Moreover, all the earth came to Egypt to Joseph to buy grain, because the famine was severe over all the earth.

Luke 14:28-30 — "For which of you, desiring to build a tower, does not first sit down and count the cost, whether he has enough to complete it? Otherwise, when he has laid a foundation, and is not able to finish, all who see it begin to mock him, saying, 'This man began to build, and was not able to finish.'"

BIBLE AND *CATECHISM* REFERENCES — SESSION SIX

Discussion Topic 1

Genesis 41 — See Appendix A, Bible and *Catechism* References – Session Five, Discussion Topic 4.

Discussion Topic 2

1 Timothy 6:9-10 — But those who desire to be rich fall into temptation, into a snare, into many senseless and hurtful desires that plunge men into ruin and destruction. For the love of money is the root of all evils; it is through this craving that some have wandered away from the faith and pierced their hearts with many pangs.

Matthew 25:14-30 — "For it will be as when a man going on a journey called his servants and entrusted to them his property; to one he gave five talents, to another two, to another one, to each according to his ability. Then he went away. He who had received the five talents went at once and traded with them; and he made five talents more. So also, he who had the two talents made two talents more. But he who had received the one talent went and dug in the ground and hid his master's money. Now after a long time the master of those servants came and settled accounts with them. And he who had received the five talents came forward, bringing five talents more, saying, 'Master, you delivered to me five talents; here I have made five talents more.' His master said to him, 'Well done, good and faithful servant; you have been faithful over a little, I will set you over much; enter into the joy of your master.' And he also who had the two talents came forward, saying, 'Master, you delivered to me two talents; here I have made two talents more.' His master said to him, 'Well done, good and faithful servant; you have been faithful over a little, I will set you over much; enter into the joy of your master.' He also who had received the one talent came forward, saying, 'Master, I knew you to be a hard man, reaping where you did not sow, and gathering where you did not winnow; so I was afraid, and I went and hid your talent in the ground. Here you have what is yours.' But his master answered him, 'You wicked and slothful servant! You knew that I reap where I have not sowed, and gather where I have not winnowed? Then you ought to have invested my money with the bankers, and at my coming I should have received what was my own with interest. So take the talent from him, and give it to him who has the ten talents. For to every one who has will more be given, and he will have abundance; but from him who has not, even what he has will be taken away. And cast the worthless servant into the outer darkness; there men will weep and gnash their teeth.'"

Proverbs 21:20 — Precious treasure remains in a wise man's dwelling, but a foolish man devours it.

Luke 12:16-21 — And he told them a parable, saying, "The land of a rich man brought forth plentifully; and he thought to himself, 'What shall I do, for I have nowhere to store my crops?' And he said, 'I will do this: I will pull down my barns, and build larger ones; and there I will store all my grain and my goods. And I will say to my soul, Soul, you have ample goods laid up for many years; take your ease, eat, drink, be merry.' But God said to him, 'Fool! This night your soul is required of you; and the things you have prepared, whose will they be?' So is he who lays up treasure for himself, and is not rich toward God."

Discussion Topic 5

Proverbs 13:11 — Wealth hastily gotten will dwindle, but he who gathers little by little will increase it.

Proverbs 21:5 — The plans of the diligent lead surely to abundance, but every one who is hasty comes only to want.

Proverbs 28:20 — A faithful man will abound with blessings, but he who hastens to be rich will not go unpunished.

Proverbs 28:22 — A miserly man hastens after wealth, and does not know that want will come upon him.

Catechism 2413 — *Games of chance* (card games, etc.) or *wagers* are not in themselves contrary to justice. They become morally unacceptable when they deprive someone of what is necessary to provide for his needs and those of others. The passion for gambling risks becoming an enslavement. Unfair wagers and cheating at games constitute grave matter, unless the damage inflicted is so slight that the one who suffers it cannot reasonably consider it significant.

Discussion Topic 6

Proverbs 27:23 — Know well the condition of your flocks, and give attention to your herds.

DISCUSSION TOPIC ANSWER KEY

*T*he purpose of this answer key is to provide key points for each of the discussion topics that ideally would be part of your answer. These answers do not cover all of the issues in depth, and certainly you'll be including your own life experiences in your personal answers. Use this as a guide to make sure you are grasping the core principles.

SESSION ONE

1. God's plan emphasizes how our attitude toward money impacts our relationship with Him and our hope of eternal life with Him. The world's plan emphasizes the here and now, and the pursuit of happiness through the accumulation of wealth and possessions. True happiness always leads back to God.

2. God's role is described as creator and owner. My role is described as a steward, or manager. A steward recognizes that he is managing resources on behalf of another. In this case, God has entrusted us to manage his resources in ways pleasing to him. What does that mean by way of priorities? Simply put, we should be doing his will, which is manifested in the Bible and Church teaching. Proper priorities would include using resources to take care of our families, help meet the needs of those less fortunate than we are, and to grow God's Kingdom here on earth by supporting the Church and her works.

3. The Lord makes it clear that there is a tension that exists between our ability to love Him as fully as we should and our attitude toward money. Unless we maintain a sense of "detachment" from our material possessions, they will interfere with our relationship with God.

4. We grow closer to the Lord by doing His will and imitating the example He gave us. As a result, we should want the goals we set in life to mirror those the Lord has given us. Our most important goal should be to spend eternity with the Lord. The path to eternity depends on our holiness, or the purity of our love for God. We show our love for God by following His instructions, including his instructions for how we manage our money. These references point us in the right direction toward holiness. It's really as simple (and as difficult) as imitating Christ and doing what He tells us. We start with the beatitudes. At the Toronto World Youth Day, Pope John Paul II called on the youth (really all of us) to be a people of the beatitudes. The Lord has given us the tools we need to become holy with the Church and the sacraments; Liturgy; the Scriptures and *Catechism*; the lives of the saints who have gone before us; and

prayer. Money touches so many areas of our lives, that it will be difficult to become as holy as we should unless we embrace a stewardship perspective.

5. It's important to remember that we all have certain strengths and weaknesses. When it comes to managing our money, we should strive to minimize the impact that our weaknesses will have on our ability to be a good steward and reach our goals. In order to do that, you need to recognize what your strengths and weaknesses are.

6. Once we recognize the capital sin that tends to be our predominant fault, it becomes possible to make great progress in our spiritual life as we make an effort to overcome or at least diminish the effect of that sin in our life. This requires spiritual exercise! The daily spiritual plan provides a consistent way for you to stay close to God's teaching and the Sacraments, and should be an integral part of your faith journey.

SESSION TWO

1. NA since the answer will be of a personal nature.

2. Just because spouses enter marriage with different perspectives toward money, there is no reason they can't develop a sense of unity. In all likelihood, the differences they have can be a real strength for their marriage, since they can draw on the best of what each other brings by way of gifts. As long as you are living out the type of married love described in Corinthians and Ephesians, you'll be assured that you are looking out for the good of the other rather than looking at the relationship in selfish terms, which is a key to maintaining unity. Finally, it's important that you remember the two of you aren't alone. Christ wants to be in the center of your marriage, and as you grow closer to Him, you'll be drawn closer to each other.

3. Once you have considered how your particular talents relate to managing your financial affairs, you'll want to determine the best way to apply them in your circumstances. If you are single and lack some of the organizational skills you feel you'll need, take steps to grow in that area. If married, it's a good idea for the spouse with the greater "bent" toward organization and detail to manage the basic financial duties.

4. Basing financial decisions on good counsel is a key to success. In the first place that counsel should come from God through prayer and reading of the Bible and other sources of Catholic teaching. If married, you should consider your spouse as your most trusted advisor after the Lord. Even though only one of you will probably be involved in the day-to-day financial basics, the "Family Budget Meeting" provides the opportunity for you to come together to share your goals and priorities in order to set a plan for the future.

5. We shouldn't be a different person at work than we are at other times. There should be a consistency to our actions based on our faith. In practical terms, this means that we'll always put our best effort forward, be honest in our dealings, follow through on commitments, be a positive influence in the workplace, and apply Catholic teaching when moral dilemmas present themselves.

6. Achieving balance in our lives is important because of the relationships involved. All relationships take time, including our walk with the Lord, our relationship with our spouse and children, and our relationships and responsibilities at work. To continue to grow in your faith, consider implementing the Daily Spiritual Plan. When it comes to your family life, set aside time each week for your spouse, whether it's by taking a walk or going out for a cup of coffee, and search for the ways that work best for interacting with your kids, whether it's tossing a ball after work, or just sitting with them and touching base about the events of the day. Use your planning and organizing skills to manage your work responsibilities effectively, and don't be afraid to delegate when appropriate. Emphasize the Church's teaching for keeping Sunday a holy day and a day of rest.

SESSION THREE

1. The key to successful child-raising is for the parents to be a good example, to pass on the principles of the faith from the early years forward, and to take an active role in the formation of their children. Parents, you need to make time for your kids – especially in today's culture. During the teen years, you'll want to give your children the opportunity to take more responsibility over financial decisions that impact them. Let them manage their own checkbook or manage their clothing budget, while still under your overall supervision. Then when they leave home, they'll be much better equipped to handle the responsibilities they will face.

2. While helping to meet various needs of the Church or assisting with the needs of the poor is a good thing, the *primary* reason we give is out of love of God and neighbor. It's really about relationships. In Malachi, the Lord says, "Return to me and I will return to you," and then calls for the Israelites to be faithful with their tithe. Jesus takes this a step further in Matthew 25, when he lets us know that when we give, we're not only helping the immediate person, we're also giving to the Lord. The verse from Corinthians sums up our motive for giving – it must be love.

3. The tithe (ten percent) was the model provided by God in the Old Testament. There were times in the history of the Israelites that it became mechanical and legalistic. This is why Jesus addresses the Pharisees in Matthew's Gospel in the way he does. He tells them to continue with the tithe, but to make it an act of the heart. The verse in 2 Corinthians further expounds on this, emphasizing that giving is now voluntary, but that we are called to be a generous people. St. Irenaeus captures this new way of thinking well. No longer does the Lord receive a tenth of what we have – he receives it all. That's really what being a "Steward of Providence" is all about. All of our resources are to be used in a manner pleasing to the Lord – certainly to meet the direct responsibilities he has given us, but also to be generous in building up his Kingdom and in showing our love for those less fortunate than we are. With American Catholics giving at a rate of one percent, it's difficult to not conclude that in many ways our giving is being done as an afterthought rather than from our "first fruits," with negative ramifications for our relationship with the Lord.

4. Tithing provides a way of recognizing God's goodness to us for the many gifts he has given. When we give generously, we establish a relationship with the Lord based on trusting that He knows what is best for us and will take care of us. It's the relationship between a perfectly loving Father and His child.

5. The letters from Mary Young emphasized the importance of integrating our faith with how we handle money. She expressed how living within one's means, avoiding debt, maintaining unity in the marriage relationship, budgeting, learning to be generous, and leading a life of prayer brings true contentment.

SESSION FOUR

1. Being a "Steward of Providence" provides the foundation for all of your financial decisions. We need to remember that God's role is creator and owner. Our role is that of a steward, or manager. Your attitude will be 90% of the reason you succeed in becoming truly financially free. By being a good steward, you make sure your financial goals are driven by your life's goals and not the other way around.

2. If you take a trip without a map, you may find that you have trouble reaching your destination. The same is true with your finances. The budget (Balance Sheet, Summary of Debts, and Veritas Budget Worksheet) acts as the map for your financial journey. Too many people assume if they balance their checkbook, they're doing all they need to, but the checkbook doesn't summarize your financial information in a way that helps you understand and set priorities. Completing a budget helps you understand where you are in the seven-step process and what steps you need to take to continue on your journey. The guideline budget helps you get started and incorporates the principles of being a good steward.

3. Establishing a budget is only a first step, although a very important one! Chances are if you are new at this, your first budget will have a number of "holes" that you'll only be able to fill by tracking your actual activity. Tracking your income and expenses gives you the information you need to budget with confidence and makes it easier to adjust for life changes that occur on the way. This will take practice and you'll get better at it over time.

4. Whenever debt is mentioned in the Bible, it has a negative connotation. Debtors are viewed as being in slavery whose assets are always at risk of being lost.

5. You can safely use credit cards if you have a balanced budget, only use them for budgeted items and pay off the entire balance every month. If you find you habitually can't pay the entire balance off each month, you would be better off closing the accounts and destroying the cards.

6. As part of your overall financial plan, you'll want to make the repayment of debt a priority, especially consumer credit (credit cards, installment loans, and auto loans, for example). You will use the Accelerator Repayment Plan to do this. Once those debts are eliminated you can consider prepaying your home loans and student loans if applicable.

7. It is very important that life insurance and estate planning needs be properly met once you have children, because of the vulnerability of your family during the children's young years.

Life insurance is designed to provide adequate resources for a family in the event of an early death of one or both of the spouses. Proper estate planning allows you to instruct how your resources will be allocated in the event of your death. In addition, it's critical to consider guardianship needs for your children in your estate plans. You'll want them to be in the hands of someone who will raise them with your same values. It's not unusual for larger families to be creating a period of dependency for 40 years or so. Proper insurance and estate planning is an important part of taking this responsibility seriously.

SESSION FIVE

1. One of the most common problems people face when it comes to their finances is that they have purchased more home than they can truly afford. As a result, they are forced to reduce their spending in other areas fairly dramatically. Unfortunately, a number of these areas are high priorities, including giving, educating children, saving for retirement and having appropriate insurance coverage. The guideline budget suggests that all housing related costs be about 30% of your gross income. This can be difficult to do, especially in certain metropolitan areas, but the more your total housing expenses exceed that figure, the more likely you'll have difficulty balancing out the important priorities in your budget.

2. Prepaying the mortgage on your home not only gets you out of debt more quickly – often by as much as fifteen years – but it also saves you tens of thousands of dollars in interest. If your mortgage is paid off by the time your children enter the college years, an added benefit is that the amount that had been allocated to your mortgage payment each year can now be used to pay for college expenses. Prepaying your mortgage is typically very simple. It's just a matter of setting a goal for when you want the mortgage to be paid off and making the corresponding higher payment. The Accelerator Repayment Plan calculator at www.VeritasFinancialMinistries.com can help you in this exercise. Remember to check with your lender to make sure there are no prepayment penalties associated with your loan.

3. Using a home equity loan to pay off old credit card debts is typically a temporary solution for most people. They are covering over the problem with a band-aid, but not addressing the underlying issue of overspending. Without changing the underlying behavior, they'll find themselves back in credit card debt in a few years, but now without the hard earned equity they should have had. Home equity loans also lead to people paying more in interest because they will take much longer to pay the debts down. Except for limited circumstances, using a home equity loan to make home improvements tends to squeeze the remainder of the budget as overall housing costs move up from the suggested 30% figure noted in question seven. You'd be better off to save for the needed improvements and pay cash.

4. Remember that a steward is a manager. We are managers over *all* of the gifts the Lord has given us. It is true that developing a generous spirit and giving of our resources is an important part of this responsibility, but managing the remaining part in ways pleasing to the Lord is just as important.

5. Spend according to your plan; comparison shop – develop a price list; don't get caught up with brand images; buy used when it makes sense; sleep on the big decisions.

SESSION SIX

1. Certain needs in the future, such as college and retirement, require saving money today in order to have the resources you'll need at the appropriate time. With the cost of a college education rising, most families will not be able to fund the expense fully from their income at the time. With retirement, you can't count on a salary from working, so you need to save up enough so that the earnings from your savings is sufficient to meet your needs. In addition, we can all expect to have times of "famine," where life throws us a curve that we didn't expect. We should have savings set aside for such times. This is the lesson from the story of Joseph in Genesis 41.

2. The Bible instructs us to achieve balance when it comes to our savings decisions. We should save for future needs, but not to the point that we are hoarding. One of the ways to bring balance to this area is to go through the exercise of determining your anticipated future needs, such as educating your children and retirement. If you are blessed with adequate resources to meet these needs, you should then consider how the Lord might be calling you to use your additional resources.

3. When money is saved and invested properly, it grows over time. It is this growth effect from compound earnings that will help you save enough for your future needs. On the flip side, if you are paying high interest rates for consumer loans, the effect of compound interest is working against you.

4. Most people will share the common goals of owning a home, helping their children receive a solid education, and meeting their needs for retirement. If you are going to save adequately today so that you can reach these goals, you need to live *below* your income, probably by about 10-15% (saving 10-15% of your gross income is a good generic goal). The best step you can take to understand whether you can save for the future is to establish a budget that reflects saving as a priority. Your budget may show that you need to look at reducing other expenses that are not as high a priority as savings is.

5. Trying to get rich quick is one of the easy ways to lose your money quickly. Remember the old saying, "If it sounds too good to be true, it probably is." Successfully saving and investing is a long term process and requires patience. Remember too that gambling can easily become an addiction and can have long-term harmful consequences not only for the gambler, but for those closest to him.

6. Mutual funds offer a good investment path for a variety of reasons, including professional fund management and proper diversification. Monitoring the performance of your investments is the only way to see if you are on track to meet your goals. Periodic reviews allow you to make necessary adjustments as your life's circumstances change and to weed out poor performing investments. Key investment measures include year-to-date return, fund expense ratio, and historical returns over the last 3, 5 and 10 years.

PRAYER JOURNAL

THE IMPORTANCE OF PRAYER

*I*n Philippians 4:6, we read, "Have no anxiety about anything, but in everything by prayer and supplication with thanksgiving let your requests be made known to God."

During this small-group study, your leader will give you the opportunity to share needs that you would like your group to keep in prayer. Use the accompanying Prayer Journals to write down the prayer intentions of your fellow group members. Use one journal page for each single person or couple in the group. Prayer is powerful, and during the course of the six week study, you are also encouraged to share how the Lord has answered your prayers.

Daily Prayer Journal

PHILIPPIANS 4:6

Names

_____ Birthday: ___/___/____

_____ Birthday: ___/___/____

Children and Ages

_____ (___) _____ (___)

_____ (___) _____ (___)

_____ (___) _____ (___)

_____ (___) _____ (___)

Home / Mobile / Office Phone Numbers

(_____) _____-_____ (H)

(_____) _____-_____ (M)

(_____) _____-_____ (O)

E-mail Address

_____@ _____

Home Address:

Street:_____

City: _____ State: _____ Zip: _____

PRAYER INTENTIONS	ANSWERS	WEEK
		0
		1
		2
		3
		4
		5
		6
Continuing Prayer Intentions		C

Daily Prayer Journal

PHILIPPIANS 4:6

Names	
_____Birthday: ___/___/___	
_____Birthday: ___/___/___	

Home / Mobile / Office Phone Numbers
(_____) _____-_____ (H)
(_____) _____-_____ (M)
(_____) _____-_____ (O)

Children and Ages	
_____ (____) _____ (____)	
_____ (____) _____ (____)	
_____ (____) _____ (____)	
_____ (____) _____ (____)	

E-mail Address

_____@ _____

Home Address:

Street:_____

City: _____ State: _____ Zip: _____

PRAYER INTENTIONS	ANSWERS	WEEK
		0
		1
		2
		3
		4
		5
		6
Continuing Prayer Intentions		G

Daily Prayer Journal

PHILIPPIANS 4:6

Names		Home / Mobile / Office Phone Numbers	
_____Birthday: ___/___/___		(_____) _____-_____ (H)	
_____Birthday: ___/___/___		(_____) _____-_____ (M)	
		(_____) _____-_____ (O)	

Children and Ages

_____ (___) _____ (___)

_____ (___) _____ (___)

_____ (___) _____ (___)

_____ (___) _____ (___)

E-mail Address

_____@ _____

Home Address:

Street:_____

City: _____ State: _____ Zip: _____

PRAYER INTENTIONS	ANSWERS	WEEK
		0
		1
		2
		3
		4
		5
		6
Continuing Prayer Intentions		C

Daily Prayer Journal

PHILIPPIANS 4:6

Names		Home / Mobile / Office Phone Numbers

_____ Birthday: ___/___/___

_____ Birthday: ___/___/___

(_____) _____-_____ (H)

(_____) _____-_____ (M)

(_____) _____-_____ (O)

Children and Ages		E-mail Address

_____ (____) _____ (____)

_____ (____) _____ (____)

_____ (____) _____ (____)

_____ (____) _____ (____)

_____@_____

Home Address:

Street:_____

City: _____ State: _____ Zip: _____

PRAYER INTENTIONS	ANSWERS	WEEK
		0
		1
		2
		3
		4
		5
		6
Continuing Prayer Intentions		C

Daily Prayer Journal

PHILIPPIANS 4:6

Names

_____ Birthday: ___/___/____

_____ Birthday: ___/___/____

Children and Ages

_____ (___) _____ (___)

_____ (___) _____ (___)

_____ (___) _____ (___)

_____ (___) _____ (___)

Home / Mobile / Office Phone Numbers

(_____) _____-_____ (H)

(_____) _____-_____ (M)

(_____) _____-_____ (O)

E-mail Address

_____@ _____

Home Address:

Street:_____

City: _____ State: _____ Zip: _____

PRAYER INTENTIONS	ANSWERS	WEEK
		0
		1
		2
		3
		4
		5
		6
Continuing Prayer Intentions		G

Daily Prayer Journal

PHILIPPIANS 4:6

Names

_____ Birthday: ___/___/____

_____ Birthday: ___/___/____

Children and Ages

_____ (   ) _____ (___)

_____ (___) _____ (___)

_____ (___) _____ (___)

_____ (___) _____ (___)

Home / Mobile / Office Phone Numbers

(_____) _____-_____ (H)

(_____) _____-_____ (M)

(_____) _____-_____ (O)

E-mail Address

_____@_____

Home Address:

Street:_____

City: _____ State: _____ Zip: _____

PRAYER INTENTIONS	ANSWERS	WEEK
		0
		1
		2
		3
		4
		5
		6
Continuing Prayer Intentions		C

Daily Prayer Journal

PHILIPPIANS 4:6

Names

_____Birthday: ___/___/___

_____Birthday: ___/___/___

Home / Mobile / Office Phone Numbers

(_____) _____-_____ (H)

(_____) _____-_____ (M)

(_____) _____-_____ (O)

Children and Ages

_____ (___) _____ (___)

_____ (___) _____ (___)

_____ (___) _____ (___)

_____ (___) _____ (___)

E-mail Address

_____@ _____

Home Address:

Street:_____

City: _____ State: _____ Zip: _____

PRAYER INTENTIONS	ANSWERS	WEEK
		0
		1
		2
		3
		4
		5
		6
Continuing Prayer Intentions		C

Daily Prayer Journal

PHILIPPIANS 4:6

Names

_____Birthday: ___/___/____

_____Birthday: ___/___/____

Home / Mobile / Office Phone Numbers

(_____) _____-_____ (H)

(_____) _____-_____ (M)

(_____) _____-_____ (O)

Children and Ages

_____ (___) _____ (___)

_____ (___) _____ (___)

_____ (___) _____ (___)

_____ (___) _____ (___)

E-mail Address

_____@ _____

Home Address:

Street:_____

City: _____ State: _____ Zip: _____

PRAYER INTENTIONS	ANSWERS	WEEK
		0
		1
		2
		3
		4
		5
		6
Continuing Prayer Intentions		C

Daily Prayer Journal

PHILIPPIANS 4:6

Names

_____Birthday: ___/___/____

_____Birthday: ___/___/____

Children and Ages

_____ (___)_____ (___)

_____ (___)_____ (___)

_____ (___)_____ (___)

_____ (___)_____ (___)

Home / Mobile / Office Phone Numbers

(_____) _____-_____ (H)

(_____) _____-_____ (M)

(_____) _____-_____ (O)

E-mail Address

_____@ _____

Home Address:

Street:_____

City: _____ State: _____ Zip: _____

PRAYER INTENTIONS	ANSWERS	WEEK
		0
		1
		2
		3
		4
		5
		6
Continuing Prayer Intentions		G

Daily Prayer Journal

PHILIPPIANS 4:6

Names

_____ Birthday: ___/___/____

_____ Birthday: ___/___/____

Home / Mobile / Office Phone Numbers

(_____) _____-_____ (H)

(_____) _____-_____ (M)

(_____) _____-_____ (O)

Children and Ages

_____ (___) _____ (___)

_____ (___) _____ (___)

_____ (___) _____ (___)

_____ (___) _____ (___)

E-mail Address

_____@ _____

Home Address:

Street:_____

City: _____ State: _____ Zip: _____

PRAYER INTENTIONS	ANSWERS	WEEK
		0
		1
		2
		3
		4
		5
		6
Continuing Prayer Intentions		C

Daily Prayer Journal

PHILIPPIANS 4:6

Names

_____Birthday: ___/___/___

_____Birthday: ___/___/___

Children and Ages

_____ (___) _____ (___)

_____ (___) _____ (___)

_____ (___) _____ (___)

_____ (___) _____ (___)

Home / Mobile / Office Phone Numbers

(_____) _____-_____ (H)

(_____) _____-_____ (M)

(_____) _____-_____ (O)

E-mail Address

_____@_____

Home Address:

Street:_____

City: _____ State: _____ Zip: _____

PRAYER INTENTIONS	ANSWERS	WEEK
		0
		1
		2
		3
		4
		5
		6
Continuing Prayer Intentions		C

Appendix D

TEMPLATE FINANCIAL FORMS

Note: This workbook contains three blank copies of each form. Participants are advised to remove forms from workbook and make photocopies for actual use.

SPENDING DIARY

Date	Pmt Type (Note 1)	Description	Giving	Current Education	Savings and Investments	Housing	Groceries	Transportation	Medical and Dental

Monthly Total

Multiply by 12 to annualize

Estmated Annual Expense

Note 1: (Cash; Check #; ATM; Credit Card; Bill Pay)
Note 2: If need space for more transactions continue with additional page

SPENDING DIARY

Date	Pmt Type (Note 1)	Description	Insurance	Debt Payments	Clothing	Entertainment and Recreation	Work Related	Miscellaneous

Monthly Total

Multiply by 12 to annualize

Estmated Annual Expense

Note 1: (Cash; Check #; ATM; Credit Card; Bill Pay)
Note 2: If need space for more transactions continue with additional page

SPENDING DIARY

Date	Pmt Type (Note 1)	Description	Giving	Current Education	Savings and Investments	Housing	Groceries	Transportation	Medical and Dental

Monthly Total

Multiply by 12 to annualize

Estmated Annual Expense

Note 1: (Cash; Check #; ATM; Credit Card; Bill Pay)
Note 2: If need space for more transactions continue with additional page

continued on back...

SPENDING DIARY

Date	Pmt Type (Note 1)	Description	Insurance	Debt Payments	Clothing	Entertainment and Recreation	Work Related	Miscellaneous

Monthly Total

Multiply by 12 to annualize

Estmated Annual Expense

Note 1: (Cash; Check #; ATM; Credit Card; Bill Pay)
Note 2: If need space for more transactions continue with additional page

SPENDING DIARY

Date	Pmt Type (Note 1)	Description	Giving	Current Education	Savings and Investments	Housing	Groceries	Transportation	Medical and Dental

Monthly Total

Multiply by 12 to annualize

Estimated Annual Expense

Note 1: (Cash; Check #; ATM; Credit Card; Bill Pay)
Note 2: If need space for more transactions continue with additional page

continued on back...

SPENDING DIARY

Date	Pmt Type (Note 1)	Description	Insurance	Debt Payments	Clothing	Entertainment and Recreation	Work Related	Miscellaneous

Monthly Total

Multiply by 12 to annualize

Estmated Annual Expense

Note 1: (Cash; Check #; ATM; Credit Card; Bill Pay)
Note 2: If need space for more transactions continue with additional page

BALANCE SHEET

Description	Current Year	Prior Year
ASSETS		
Cash and Cash Equivalents		
Cash on Hand		
Cash — Checking		
Cash — Money Market		
Cash — Other		
Total Cash and Cash Equivalents		
Invested Assets		
Certificates of Deposit		
Brokerage Accounts		
Retirement Plans		
Business Investment		
Total Invested Assets		
Use Assets		
House		
Autos		
Other		
Total Use Assets		
TOTAL ASSETS		
LIABILITIES		
Mortgage and Home Equity Loans		
Auto Loans		
Credit Cards and Installment Loans		
Student Loans		
Business Debt		
Other (Loans from Family and Friends; Retirement Plans; Life Insurance)		
TOTAL LIABILITIES		
NET WORTH		

BALANCE SHEET

Description	Current Year	Prior Year
ASSETS		
Cash and Cash Equivalents		
Cash on Hand		
Cash — Checking		
Cash — Money Market		
Cash — Other		
Total Cash and Cash Equivalents		
Invested Assets		
Certificates of Deposit		
Brokerage Accounts		
Retirement Plans		
Business Investment		
Total Invested Assets		
Use Assets		
House		
Autos		
Other		
Total Use Assets		
TOTAL ASSETS		
LIABILITIES		
Mortgage and Home Equity Loans		
Auto Loans		
Credit Cards and Installment Loans		
Student Loans		
Business Debt		
Other (Loans from Family and Friends; Retirement Plans; Life Insurance)		
TOTAL LIABILITIES		
NET WORTH		

BALANCE SHEET

Description	Current Year	Prior Year
ASSETS		
Cash and Cash Equivalents		
Cash on Hand		
Cash — Checking		
Cash — Money Market		
Cash — Other		
Total Cash and Cash Equivalents		
Invested Assets		
Certificates of Deposit		
Brokerage Accounts		
Retirement Plans		
Business Investment		
Total Invested Assets		
Use Assets		
House		
Autos		
Other		
Total Use Assets		
TOTAL ASSETS		
LIABILITIES		
Mortgage and Home Equity Loans		
Auto Loans		
Credit Cards and Installment Loans		
Student Loans		
Business Debt		
Other (Loans from Family and Friends; Retirement Plans; Life Insurance)		
TOTAL LIABILITIES		
NET WORTH		

SUMMARY OF DEBTS—MORTGAGE AND AUTO

Type of Debt	To Whom Owed	Balance Due	# of Payments Remaining	Interest Rate	Min Required Monthly Payment	# Months Past Due	Describe What Was Purchased
Mortgage/ Home Equity	Name: Address: City: State: Zip: Telephone:						
Mortgage/ Home Equity	Name: Address: City: State: Zip: Telephone:						
Total Mortgage/Home Equity							
Auto	Name: Address: City: State: Zip: Telephone:						
Auto	Name: Address: City: State: Zip: Telephone:						
Auto	Name: Address: City: State: Zip: Telephone:						
Total Auto							

Page 1 of 4—continued on back . . . .

SUMMARY OF DEBTS—CREDIT CARDS

Type of Debt	To Whom Owed	Balance Due	# of Payments Remaining	Interest Rate	Min Required Monthly Payment	# Months Past Due	Describe What Was Purchased
Credit Card	Name: Address: City: State: Zip: Telephone:						
Credit Card	Name: Address: City: State: Zip: Telephone:						
Credit Card	Name: Address: City: State: Zip: Telephone:						
Credit Card	Name: Address: City: State: Zip: Telephone:						
Credit Card	Name: Address: City: State: Zip: Telephone:						

Total Credit Cards/Installment

Page 2 of 4—continued on next page . . . .

SUMMARY OF DEBTS—STUDENT AND BUSINESS DEBTS

Type of Debt	To Whom Owed	Balance Due	# of Payments Remaining	Interest Rate	Min Required Monthly Payment	# Months Past Due	Describe What Was Purchased
Student Loan	Name: Address: City: State: Zip: Telephone:						
Student Loan	Name: Address: City: State: Zip: Telephone:						
Student Loan	Name: Address: City: State: Zip: Telephone:						
Total Student Loans							
Business Debt	Name: Address: City: State: Zip: Telephone:						
Business Debt	Name: Address: City: State: Zip: Telephone:						
Total Business Debt							

Page 3 of 4—continued on back....

SUMMARY OF DEBTS—OTHER DEBTS

Type of Debt	To Whom Owed	Balance Due	# of Payments Remaining	Interest Rate	Min Required Monthly Payment	# Months Past Due	Describe What Was Purchased
Other	Name: Address: City: State: Zip: Telephone:						
Other	Name: Address: City: State: Zip: Telephone:						
Other	Name: Address: City: State: Zip: Telephone:						
Other	Name: Address: City: State: Zip: Telephone:						
Other	Name: Address: City: State: Zip: Telephone:						

Total Other Debts

SUMMARY OF DEBTS—MORTGAGE AND AUTO

Type of Debt	To Whom Owed	Balance Due	# of Payments Remaining	Interest Rate	Min Required Monthly Payment	# Months Past Due	Describe What Was Purchased
Mortgage/ Home Equity	Name: Address: City: State: Zip: Telephone:						
Mortgage/ Home Equity	Name: Address: City: State: Zip: Telephone:						
Total Mortgage/Home Equity							
Auto	Name: Address: City: State: Zip: Telephone:						
Auto	Name: Address: City: State: Zip: Telephone:						
Auto	Name: Address: City: State: Zip: Telephone:						
Total Auto							

Page 1 of 4—continued on back....

SUMMARY OF DEBTS—CREDIT CARDS

Type of Debt	To Whom Owed	Balance Due	# of Payments Remaining	Interest Rate	Min Required Monthly Payment	# Months Past Due	Describe What Was Purchased
Credit Card	Name: Address: City: State: Zip: Telephone:						
Credit Card	Name: Address: City: State: Zip: Telephone:						
Credit Card	Name: Address: City: State: Zip: Telephone:						
Credit Card	Name: Address: City: State: Zip: Telephone:						
Credit Card	Name: Address: City: State: Zip: Telephone:						
Total Credit Cards/Installment							

Page 2 of 4—continued on next page . . . .

SUMMARY OF DEBTS—STUDENT AND BUSINESS DEBTS

Type of Debt	To Whom Owed	Balance Due	# of Payments Remaining	Interest Rate	Min Required Monthly Payment	# Months Past Due	Describe What Was Purchased
Student Loan	Name: Address: City: State: Zip: Telephone:						
Student Loan	Name: Address: City: State: Zip: Telephone:						
Student Loan	Name: Address: City: State: Zip: Telephone:						
Total Student Loans							
Business Debt	Name: Address: City: State: Zip: Telephone:						
Business Debt	Name: Address: City: State: Zip: Telephone:						
Total Business Debt							

Page 3 of 4—continued on back . . . .

SUMMARY OF DEBTS—OTHER DEBTS

Type of Debt	To Whom Owed	Balance Due	# of Payments Remaining	Interest Rate	Min Required Monthly Payment	# Months Past Due	Describe What Was Purchased
Other	Name: Address: City: State: Zip: Telephone:						
Other	Name: Address: City: State: Zip: Telephone:						
Other	Name: Address: City: State: Zip: Telephone:						
Other	Name: Address: City: State: Zip: Telephone:						
Other	Name: Address: City: State: Zip: Telephone:						

Total Other Debts

SUMMARY OF DEBTS—MORTGAGE AND AUTO

Type of Debt	To Whom Owed	Balance Due	# of Payments Remaining	Interest Rate	Min Required Monthly Payment	# Months Past Due	Describe What Was Purchased
Mortgage/ Home Equity	Name: Address: City: State: Zip: Telephone:						
Mortgage/ Home Equity	Name: Address: City: State: Zip: Telephone:						
Total Mortgage/Home Equity							
Auto	Name: Address: City: State: Zip: Telephone:						
Auto	Name: Address: City: State: Zip: Telephone:						
Auto	Name: Address: City: State: Zip: Telephone:						
Total Auto							

Page 1 of 4—continued on back....

SUMMARY OF DEBTS—CREDIT CARDS

Type of Debt	To Whom Owed	Balance Due	# of Payments Remaining	Interest Rate	Min Required Monthly Payment	# Months Past Due	Describe What Was Purchased
Credit Card	Name: Address: City: State: Zip: Telephone:						
Credit Card	Name: Address: City: State: Zip: Telephone:						
Credit Card	Name: Address: City: State: Zip: Telephone:						
Credit Card	Name: Address: City: State: Zip: Telephone:						
Credit Card	Name: Address: City: State: Zip: Telephone:						
Total Credit Cards/Installment							

Page 2 of 4—continued on next page . . . .

SUMMARY OF DEBTS—STUDENT AND BUSINESS DEBTS

Type of Debt	To Whom Owed	Balance Due	# of Payments Remaining	Interest Rate	Min Required Monthly Payment	# Months Past Due	Describe What Was Purchased
Student Loan	Name: Address: City: State: Zip: Telephone:						
Student Loan	Name: Address: City: State: Zip: Telephone:						
Student Loan	Name: Address: City: State: Zip: Telephone:						
Total Student Loans							
Business Debt	Name: Address: City: State: Zip: Telephone:						
Business Debt	Name: Address: City: State: Zip: Telephone:						
Total Business Debt							

Page 3 of 4—continued on back....

FORM C — SUMMARY OF DEBTS P3   137

SUMMARY OF DEBTS—OTHER DEBTS

Type of Debt	To Whom Owed	Balance Due	# of Payments Remaining	Interest Rate	Min Required Monthly Payment	# Months Past Due	Describe What Was Purchased
Other	Name: Address: City: State: Zip: Telephone:						
Other	Name: Address: City: State: Zip: Telephone:						
Other	Name: Address: City: State: Zip: Telephone:						
Other	Name: Address: City: State: Zip: Telephone:						
Other	Name: Address: City: State: Zip: Telephone:						

Total Other Debts

GUIDELINE BUDGET REVIEW

Account Description	Estimated Annual Income/Expenses	Actual Annual %	Guideline Budget	Guideline Budget %
Gross Income		100%		100%
Salary				
Bonus				
Interest				
Dividends				
Retirement Plan				
Other				
Tithe/Giving				
Deductible				
Non-deductible				
Children Tuition				
Taxes				
Federal Income				
State Income				
Social Security				
Medicare				
State Disability				
Current Education				
Tuition (See tithe)				
Supplies				
Day Care				
Other				
Savings				
Emergency and Rainy Day				
Future Education				
Retirement Plan				
Housing and Home Expenses				
Mortgage/rent				
Insurance				
Taxes				
Electricity				
Gas				
Water				
Gardening				
Housecleaning				
Telephone				
Maintenance				
Pest Control				
Association Dues				
Bottled Water				
Postage				
Miscellaneous				
Improvements				
Groceries				

continued on back...

GUIDELINE BUDGET REVIEW continued

Account Description	Estimated Annual Income/Expenses	Actual Annual %	Guideline Budget	Guideline Budget %
Transportation				
Payment/Replace Savings				
Gas/Oil				
Insurance				
License/Taxes				
Maintenance/Repair				
Medical Expenses				
Doctor				
Dentist				
Prescriptions				
Other				
Insurance				
Medical				
Life				
Disability				
Debt Payments				
Credit Card				
Loans and Notes				
Other				
Clothing				
Entertain. and Recreation				
Eating Out				
Babysitting				
Cable/Satellite/Movies				
Allowances				
Activities				
Vacation				
Work Related				
Education/Dues				
Internet/Phone				
Other				
Miscellaneous				
Beauty/Barber/Cosmetics				
Laundry				
Subscriptions				
Holiday/Gifts				
Accounting/Legal				
Veterinarian/Animals				
Summary of Inc./Exp.				
Total Income				
Total Expenses				
Income Over/(Under) Exp.				

GUIDELINE BUDGET REVIEW

Account Description	Estimated Annual Income/Expenses	Actual Annual %	Guideline Budget	Guideline Budget %
Gross Income		100%		100%
Salary				
Bonus				
Interest				
Dividends				
Retirement Plan				
Other				
Tithe/Giving				
Deductible				
Non-deductible				
Children Tuition				
Taxes				
Federal Income				
State Income				
Social Security				
Medicare				
State Disability				
Current Education				
Tuition (See tithe)				
Supplies				
Day Care				
Other				
Savings				
Emergency and Rainy Day				
Future Education				
Retirement Plan				
Housing and Home Expenses				
Mortgage/rent				
Insurance				
Taxes				
Electricity				
Gas				
Water				
Gardening				
Housecleaning				
Telephone				
Maintenance				
Pest Control				
Association Dues				
Bottled Water				
Postage				
Miscellaneous				
Improvements				
Groceries				

continued on back...

GUIDELINE BUDGET REVIEW continued

Account Description	Estimated Annual Income/Expenses	Actual Annual %	Guideline Budget	Guideline Budget %
Transportation				
Payment/Replace Savings				
Gas/Oil				
Insurance				
License/Taxes				
Maintenance/Repair				
Medical Expenses				
Doctor				
Dentist				
Prescriptions				
Other				
Insurance				
Medical				
Life				
Disability				
Debt Payments				
Credit Card				
Loans and Notes				
Other				
Clothing				
Entertain. and Recreation				
Eating Out				
Babysitting				
Cable/Satellite/Movies				
Allowances				
Activities				
Vacation				
Work Related				
Education/Dues				
Internet/Phone				
Other				
Miscellaneous				
Beauty/Barber/Cosmetics				
Laundry				
Subscriptions				
Holiday/Gifts				
Accounting/Legal				
Veterinarian/Animals				
Summary of Inc./Exp.				
Total Income				
Total Expenses				
Income Over/(Under) Exp.				

GUIDELINE BUDGET REVIEW

Account Description	Estimated Annual Income/Expenses	Actual Annual %	Guideline Budget	Guideline Budget %
Gross Income		100%		100%
Salary				
Bonus				
Interest				
Dividends				
Retirement Plan				
Other				
Tithe/Giving				
Deductible				
Non-deductible				
Children Tuition				
Taxes				
Federal Income				
State Income				
Social Security				
Medicare				
State Disability				
Current Education				
Tuition (See tithe)				
Supplies				
Day Care				
Other				
Savings				
Emergency and Rainy Day				
Future Education				
Retirement Plan				
Housing and Home Expenses				
Mortgage/rent				
Insurance				
Taxes				
Electricity				
Gas				
Water				
Gardening				
Housecleaning				
Telephone				
Maintenance				
Pest Control				
Association Dues				
Bottled Water				
Postage				
Miscellaneous				
Improvements				
Groceries				

continued on back...

GUIDELINE BUDGET REVIEW continued

Account Description	Estimated Annual Income/Expenses	Actual Annual %	Guideline Budget	Guideline Budget %
Transportation				
Payment/Replace Savings				
Gas/Oil				
Insurance				
License/Taxes				
Maintenance/Repair				
Medical Expenses				
Doctor				
Dentist				
Prescriptions				
Other				
Insurance				
Medical				
Life				
Disability				
Debt Payments				
Credit Card				
Loans and Notes				
Other				
Clothing				
Entertain. and Recreation				
Eating Out				
Babysitting				
Cable/Satellite/Movies				
Allowances				
Activities				
Vacation				
Work Related				
Education/Dues				
Internet/Phone				
Other				
Miscellaneous				
Beauty/Barber/Cosmetics				
Laundry				
Subscriptions				
Holiday/Gifts				
Accounting/Legal				
Veterinarian/Animals				
Summary of Inc./Exp.				
Total Income				
Total Expenses				
Income Over/(Under) Exp.				

VERITAS BUDGET WORKSHEET

Account Description	Year-to-date Income/Expenses	Actual Annual %	Annual Budget	Annual Budget %
Gross Income		100%		100%
Salary				
Bonus				
Interest				
Dividends				
Retirement Plan				
Other				
Tithe/Giving				
Deductible				
Non-deductible				
Children Tuition				
Taxes				
Federal Income				
State Income				
Social Security				
Medicare				
State Disability				
Current Education				
Tuition (See tithe)				
Supplies				
Day Care				
Other				
Savings				
Emergency and Rainy Day				
Future Education				
Retirement Plan				
Housing and Home Expenses				
Mortgage/rent				
Insurance				
Taxes				
Electricity				
Gas				
Water				
Gardening				
Housecleaning				
Telephone				
Maintenance				
Pest Control				
Association Dues				
Bottled Water				
Postage				
Miscellaneous				
Improvements				
Groceries				

continued on back...

Account Description	Year-to-date Income/Expenses	Actual Annual %	Annual Budget	Annual Budget %
VERITAS BUDGET WORKSHEET continued				
Transportation				
Payment/Replace Savings				
Gas/Oil				
Insurance				
License/Taxes				
Maintenance/Repair				
Medical Expenses				
Doctor				
Dentist				
Prescriptions				
Other				
Insurance				
Medical				
Life				
Disability				
Debt Payments				
Credit Card				
Loans and Notes				
Other				
Clothing				
Entertain. and Recreation				
Eating Out				
Babysitting				
Cable/Satellite/Movies				
Allowances				
Activities				
Vacation				
Work Related				
Education/Dues				
Internet/Phone				
Other				
Miscellaneous				
Beauty/Barber/Cosmetics				
Laundry				
Subscriptions				
Holiday/Gifts				
Accounting/Legal				
Veterinarian/Animals				
Summary of Inc./Exp.				
Total Income				
Total Expenses				
Income Over/(Under) Exp.				

VERITAS BUDGET WORKSHEET

Account Description	Year-to-date Income/Expenses	Actual Annual %	Annual Budget	Annual Budget %
Gross Income		100%		100%
Salary				
Bonus				
Interest				
Dividends				
Retirement Plan				
Other				
Tithe/Giving				
Deductible				
Non-deductible				
Children Tuition				
Taxes				
Federal Income				
State Income				
Social Security				
Medicare				
State Disability				
Current Education				
Tuition (See tithe)				
Supplies				
Day Care				
Other				
Savings				
Emergency and Rainy Day				
Future Education				
Retirement Plan				
Housing and Home Expenses				
Mortgage/rent				
Insurance				
Taxes				
Electricity				
Gas				
Water				
Gardening				
Housecleaning				
Telephone				
Maintenance				
Pest Control				
Association Dues				
Bottled Water				
Postage				
Miscellaneous				
Improvements				
Groceries				

continued on back...

VERITAS BUDGET WORKSHEET continued

Account Description	Year-to-date Income/Expenses	Actual Annual %	Annual Budget	Annual Budget %
Transportation				
Payment/Replace Savings				
Gas/Oil				
Insurance				
License/Taxes				
Maintenance/Repair				
Medical Expenses				
Doctor				
Dentist				
Prescriptions				
Other				
Insurance				
Medical				
Life				
Disability				
Debt Payments				
Credit Card				
Loans and Notes				
Other				
Clothing				
Entertain. and Recreation				
Eating Out				
Babysitting				
Cable/Satellite/Movies				
Allowances				
Activities				
Vacation				
Work Related				
Education/Dues				
Internet/Phone				
Other				
Miscellaneous				
Beauty/Barber/Cosmetics				
Laundry				
Subscriptions				
Holiday/Gifts				
Accounting/Legal				
Veterinarian/Animals				
Summary of Inc./Exp.				
Total Income				
Total Expenses				
Income Over/(Under) Exp.				

VERITAS BUDGET WORKSHEET

Account Description	Year-to-date Income/Expenses	Actual Annual %	Annual Budget	Annual Budget %
Gross Income		100%		100%
Salary				
Bonus				
Interest				
Dividends				
Retirement Plan				
Other				
Tithe/Giving				
Deductible				
Non-deductible				
Children Tuition				
Taxes				
Federal Income				
State Income				
Social Security				
Medicare				
State Disability				
Current Education				
Tuition (See tithe)				
Supplies				
Day Care				
Other				
Savings				
Emergency and Rainy Day				
Future Education				
Retirement Plan				
Housing and Home Expenses				
Mortgage/rent				
Insurance				
Taxes				
Electricity				
Gas				
Water				
Gardening				
Housecleaning				
Telephone				
Maintenance				
Pest Control				
Association Dues				
Bottled Water				
Postage				
Miscellaneous				
Improvements				
Groceries				

continued on back...

VERITAS BUDGET WORKSHEET continued

Account Description	Year-to-date Income/Expenses	Actual Annual %	Annual Budget	Annual Budget %
Transportation				
Payment/Replace Savings				
Gas/Oil				
Insurance				
License/Taxes				
Maintenance/Repair				
Medical Expenses				
Doctor				
Dentist				
Prescriptions				
Other				
Insurance				
Medical				
Life				
Disability				
Debt Payments				
Credit Card				
Loans and Notes				
Other				
Clothing				
Entertain. and Recreation				
Eating Out				
Babysitting				
Cable/Satellite/Movies				
Allowances				
Activities				
Vacation				
Work Related				
Education/Dues				
Internet/Phone				
Other				
Miscellaneous				
Beauty/Barber/Cosmetics				
Laundry				
Subscriptions				
Holiday/Gifts				
Accounting/Legal				
Veterinarian/Animals				
Summary of Inc./Exp.				
Total Income				
Total Expenses				
Income Over/(Under) Exp.				

INDIVIDUAL ACCOUNT REGISTER

Account Description: _____ **Annual Budget** _____

Date	Check #	Description	Amount	Cumulative Total

INDIVIDUAL ACCOUNT REGISTER

Account Description: _____ **Annual Budget** _____

Date	Check #	Description	Amount	Cumulative Total

INDIVIDUAL ACCOUNT REGISTER

Account Description: _____ **Annual Budget** _____

Date	Check #	Description	Amount	Cumulative Total

INDIVIDUAL ACCOUNT REGISTER

Account Description: _____ Annual Budget _____

Date	Check #	Description	Amount	Cumulative Total

INDIVIDUAL ACCOUNT REGISTER

Account Description: _____ **Annual Budget** _____

Date	Check #	Description	Amount	Cumulative Total

INDIVIDUAL ACCOUNT REGISTER

Account Description: _____ **Annual Budget** _____

Date	Check #	Description	Amount	Cumulative Total

BUSINESS REPLY MAIL

FIRST-CLASS MAIL   PERMIT NO. 216   TEMECULA, CA

POSTAGE WILL BE PAID BY ADDRESSEE

VERITAS FINANCIAL MINISTRIES
PO BOX 892425
TEMECULA CA 92589-9768

IIIııııIıIıIııIıIılılıIııIıIıIıIııIıIIIıIıIıIıIıII

TRI-FOLD AND MAIL — FOLD EXACTLY ALONG DOTTED LINE — DO NOT STAPLE

PARTICIPANT EVALUATION AND RECOMMENDATION FORM

Thank you for taking a moment to complete this evaluation form. Through your feedback, we can make improvements to the materials and small group study that will benefit future leaders and participants. Once you have filled out the form, you can simply tear it out and drop it in the mail (no postage is required). If you would like to help Veritas Financial Ministries save on its postage costs, you can also fill out the form online at www.VeritasFinancialMinistries.com.

MATERIAL/SMALL GROUP EVALUATION

1. Which aspect of the materials and/or small group study did you find most helpful:

   ☐ *7 Steps to Becoming Financially Free* (Book)   ☐ Discussion Topics
   ☐ *7 Steps to Becoming Financially Free Workbook*   ☐ Homework
   ☐ Video — Introductory and Practical Exercises   ☐ Small Group Prayer
   ☐ Reading from Scripture and *Catechism*

2. Please indicate how the program most impacted you:

   ☐ Grew closer in their walk with the Lord   ☐ Developed a budget
   ☐ Level of giving increased   ☐ Eliminated debt
   ☐ Increased savings   ☐ Marriage enhanced

3. Please share a testimony about how these materials and/or participating in a group study has impacted you:

   _____
   _____
   _____
   _____

4. Please provide suggestions for how the materials and/or the small group study can be improved:

   _____
   _____
   _____
   _____

TITLE: ☐ MR. ☐ MRS. ☐ MISS ☐ DR. ☐ REV. ☐ DEACON ☐ SISTER

FIRST NAME

LAST NAME

SPOUSE'S TITLE: ☐ MR. ☐ MRS. ☐ MISS ☐ DR. ☐ DEACON

SPOUSE'S FIRST NAME

SPOUSE'S LAST NAME

HOME ADDRESS

CITY

STATE   ZIP CODE   COUNTRY

HOME PHONE   WORK PHONE/MOBILE PHONE

E-MAIL ADDRESS

CHURCH/CLASS LOCATION INFORMATION

SMALL GROUP LEADER NAME

CHURCH NAME

CITY

STATE   ZIP CODE   COUNTRY

VERITAS FINANCIAL MINISTRIES E-LETTER

Phil Lenahan sends a monthly E-letter to friends of Veritas Financial Ministries. The E-letter includes helpful tips on managing your money in a Godly way and updates on the work of the ministry. Please indicate below whether you would like to receive Phil's E-letter.

☐ Yes, I would like to receive Phil's monthly E-letter from Veritas Financial Ministries.

☐ I'll add the work of Veritas Financial Ministries to my prayer intentions.

☐ I am interested in becoming a volunteer small group leader with Veritas Financial Ministries.

☐ I would like to make a donation to further the work of Veritas Financial Ministries in the amount of $_____